Bullets into Bells

D0974923

Bullets into bells :
poets & citizens respond
[2017]
33305241235740
sa   05/04/18

Bullets into Bells

Poets & Citizens
Respond to Gun Violence

D0974928

Edited by
BRIAN CLEMENTS
ALEXANDRA TEAGUE
and DEAN RADER

Introduction by
COLUM McCANN

BEACON PRESS
BOSTON

Beacon Press
Boston, Massachusetts
www.beacon.org

Beacon Press books
are published under the auspices of
the Unitarian Universalist Association of Congregations.

© 2017 Beacon Press
All rights reserved
Printed in the United States of America

Introduction © 2017 by Colum McCann

20 19 18 17   8 7 6 5 4 3 2 1

This book is printed on acid-free paper that meets the uncoated paper
ANSI/NISO specifications for permanence as revised in 1992.

Text design and composition by Michael Starkman
at Wilsted & Taylor Publishing Services

LIBRARY OF CONGRESS CATALOGING-IN-PUBLICATION DATA

Names: Clements, Brian, editor. | Teague, Alexandra, editor. |
    Rader, Dean editor.
Title: Bullets into bells : poets & citizens respond to gun violence /
    edited by Brian Clements, Alexandra Teague, and Dean Rader ;
    introduction by Colum McCann.
Description: Boston : Beacon Press, 2017.
Identifiers: LCCN 2017018375 (print) | LCCN 2017042584 (ebook) |
    ISBN 9780807025598 (e-book) | ISBN 9780807025581 (pbk. : alk. paper)
Subjects: LCSH: Gun control—Poetry. | Firearms ownership—Poetry. |
    Violent crimes—Poetry. | Mass murder—Poetry. | American poetry—
    21st century.
Classification: LCC PS595.G86 (ebook) | LCC PS595.G86 B85 2017 (print) |
    DDC 811/.60803556—dc23
LC record available at https://lccn.loc.gov/2017018375

CONTENTS

Congresswoman Gabrielle Giffords
and Captain Mark Kelly

Our country is in the grips of a gun violence crisis. It has crept into our neighborhoods, towns, cities, and states. It has created fear in spaces of joy and innocence, like movie theaters and schools. It costs our cities and towns millions of dollars and leaves holes in our communities that can never be filled. It makes our country stand out in the worst of ways.

Neither of us began our lives in public service thinking that gun violence prevention would be our life's work. But gun violence shattered our lives as we knew them, and we won't stop fighting to prevent mass shooting tragedies and the gun violence that occurs on our streets and in our homes every single day.

Survivors, advocates, and allies can change hearts and minds—and move more people to join our fight for solutions—by telling stories about the irreparable damage that gun violence does to families and communities across the country.

We're in this movement because of our personal story, and we stay committed to preventing gun violence because of stories like these.

THE VELOCITY OF LANGUAGE

Colum McCann

"If you speak, you die. If you keep quiet, you die. So, speak and die." Shortly after the Algerian poet and journalist Tahar Djaout wrote these words in the summer of 1993 he was gunned down in the streets of Algiers. Djaout spoke in favor of progress, secularism, decency, a broader world where intellectual and moral narrowness would be defeated. But the bullets did their work: after a week in a coma, Djaout died. His killers, a fundamentalist group, later admitted that they feared him because he wielded the mighty weapon of language.

The tragedy of it all was that Djaout's voice was silenced and amplified at the same time. We have no way of knowing what else Djaout would have said or how he might have shaped a different future for his part of the world. Everything at the end of a bullet's journey becomes conjecture.

Still, the fact remains that Djaout did speak out during his short life. His death had backspin. Nobody was going to be able to wipe out what he had already said. Having written, he spoke. Having spoken, he endured. Having endured, he now survives.

What Djaout believed was that a lot of things can be taken away from us—even our lives—but not our stories about those lives. Eventually, no bullet will outlast the speed and velocity of language. This notion might totter on the edge of nostalgia—after all, it seems most likely that it's better to be alive than not—but Djaout's words are worth repeating: *If you speak, you die. If you keep quiet, you die. So, speak and die.*

Poets have known about the perpetuity of language, stories, and music making since the very first days when rock was scraped against the cave wall. In the beginning was the word. Others might repress it, torture it, burn it, chain it, mangle it, but the proper flesh of language cannot be outright annihilated.

The hope—and perhaps the enduring belief of literature—is that it will present itself even more inventively than ever before.

On December 2015 the *New York Times* ran an editorial on its front page—the first time the paper had done so since June 1920, when Warren Harding landed the Republican presidential nomination—calling in no uncertain terms for the proper regulation of guns in the aftermath of a spate of shootings. The editorial, titled "The Gun Epidemic," said that legally purchased weapons designed to kill with brutal speed and efficiency were a "moral outrage and a national disgrace."

At the time of the editorial, the murders in San Bernardino had just happened. Multiple shootings in Colorado Springs had left four people dead. The anniversary of Sandy Hook was just days away. All you had to do was whisper the name of a state—Oregon, Virginia, South Carolina—and immediately another tragedy shuddered in the throat.

The newspaper sparked a heated debate in its commentary boxes, with more than seven thousand people weighing in in a matter of days. *We have elected the most cowardly human beings one could find to supposedly represent the people who elected them. Frankly as a gun owner I am appalled! I'd be happy if we could find and recover our national sanity. Kill someone with a gun, then you are shot by a firing squad the day after your convic-*

tion, you could even put it on Pay Per View and give the money to the victims [sic] *family. We need civic anger. The Amendment is not a blank check to own any type of weapon. Until you outlaw capitolism* [sic], *there will always be someone willing to sell whatever people want to buy. They [the NRA] have turned into nothing more than a sycophantic lackey of the small arms industry. I'm worried that we're losing our grip on our representative democracy.*

Newspaper commentary boxes are hardly going to turn into grand symphonic cathedrals, but what was most apparent was the rancor and outright bitterness that bubbled underneath the entries. This was a country at odds with itself. The *New York Times*'s decision to throw its front-page hat into the ring was brave, but what could have been the beginning of true national soul-searching ended up, ultimately, as an exercise in division and derision and re-division.

This became especially poignant when, weeks later, President Obama stood at a White House podium and literally shed tears while recalling the first-graders in Newtown and said that all of us need to "demand a Congress brave enough to stand up to the gun lobby's lies." What resulted afterward was a sort of embarrassed national silence that slid its way into the echo chamber of the election year. The sight of a president crying on national television was a shock to the soul. He was not shedding tears for the availability of guns, or for gun control, or the paltry legislative efforts of his own colleagues— rather he was shedding tears for twenty children and six adults who had died four years previously. Obama believed that those deaths could have been prevented by proper moral action in the political sphere. He was joining the human with the political and calling on the country to examine what Faulkner would have termed "the human heart in conflict with itself."

Obama's reaction was one of the bravest moments in recent political history. Still, nothing happened: or as close to nothing as one can get.

How with this rage shall beauty hold a plea?

What becomes increasingly apparent when talking about guns or gun awareness is that it seems—at least initially—that there is very little room for embracing lasting nuance. The gauntlet is quickly thrown down. *He said, she said. He won't, we won't. All or nothing.* Subtlety quickly gurgles down the drain hole, even for those with the best of intentions. There is very little chance for the multiple sides to come together to try to even attempt to understand one another, to find any equivalence, or balance, or redress. The scales of rhetoric get tilted immediately. There is so much at stake—not just money or pride or politics, but our actual thumping lives.

Yet, what is seldom addressed in the debate about guns and gun ownership is that the vast majority of people in this country—except for a small fringe of lunatics, homegrown and foreign both—feel the exact same way about one thing: they abhor violence. This is the common ground on which most proper-thinking people stand, whether they have a gun underneath the pillow or not. Gun control advocates and the pro-gun lobby often want the exact same thing; they just haven't figured out how they can get it *together.*

You can rack up the statistics. Every year in the United States, more than thirty thousand die from gun violence, including suicides, accidents, and assaults. Sixty percent of gun owners say they own the weapons to protect themselves against crime. Between 1968 and 2015, more than 1.5 million people were killed by shootings—more Americans than in all our wars combined. It is said that toddlers mishandling guns kill more people than terrorists do. Depending on whom you talk to, it is estimated that there are one to two guns for every person in the United States.

But eventually facts and figures begin to cloud the elemental truth. Statistics are mercenary things. They can be used in any territory we want. That 1.5 million dead can be just that, one and a half million, or you can imagine lining up every man, woman, and child in Phoenix and ask them to fall to the ground one after the other, after the other, after the other. Language itself can be a great manipulator of facts: If 60 percent of American gun owners say they possess a firearm to prevent crime, does that mean that 40 percent don't? What age is a toddler and who might have put this "fact" about terrorists into the forefront of our minds? And what exactly are "all our wars combined"?

If we are genuinely interested in changing our reality on the ground, what we really need is a deeper understanding and a hope that all our disciplines—law, science, politics, education, and, yes, poetry—can come together to create an accepted, and acceptable, truth that is, in essence, a textural truth, something we know, deep in the heart's core, happens to be true and good and right.

The nobility of poetry, says Wallace Stevens, "is a violence from within that protects us from a violence without. It is the imagination pressing back against the pressure of reality." Poetry helps us to live our lives. It offers a response to all the available evidence that the world is, in fact, a tar pit of greed and despair.

What poetry can do is untangle some of the "facts" and reveal the human tissue underneath.

The aim of this anthology—so ably and passionately put together by the editors Brian Clements, Alexandra Teague, and Dean Rader—is to try to shift the nature of the debate around guns and give voice to the effect of violence in a manner that isn't always associated with the poetic. The aim, according to Clements, is that "poets, survivors, families and friends of victims, activists, political figures, researchers, and audiences will come together to share and discuss their common ground." The book is set up in a call-and-response format, a church of the possible. True, the anthology probably does lean toward those of us who might prefer to see guns vanish from our lives, but the real emotional thrust is toward antiviolence. The poems attempt to create a community built not just of grief but of hope, too.

Many people in this book have suffered publicly, but the point of their poetry is not to whine or moan or even set things aflame but rather to communicate the intricate nuances of that suffering with others. It is a form of public sharing. Take these words. Weigh them up. Listen. Pause a while. Help reality touch justice.

It would be word-consuming and indeed disingenuous for me to point out any of the individual contributors since each and every one has a voice and a story to tell, and each tells it with rhyme and economy. There are many world-famous poets here, shouldering side-by-side with contributors who are much less known. There is a very good reason for this. It amounts to a solidarity of poetic intent. Poetry calls out for us to be inclusive. This anthology is not meant to be shelved. It is designed to be left on the seats of buses, in doctor's waiting rooms, on street corners, in order to say that we are in this together. The self-evident truth is that we need to start talking to one another, not with a legion of sound bites or statistics but with human texture and longing to at least lessen, if not eradicate, the violence that afflicts us.

One of the beauties of poetry is that it is essentially an act of nonviolence. It can make us feel the pain, but we do not necessarily have to suffer it.

In poetry and storytelling, a ritual transaction occurs between reader and writer: the reader is given an illusion that he or she suffers, or enjoys. It is a life that is not his or her own, but one the reader steps inside for a moment. We become alive in another body, or soul, or time. We are forced, in literature, to make the empathetic leap into the realm of someone else. And the stories we tell one another are our own nonviolent alternative.

I am privileged to be the cofounder, along with literary activist Lisa Consiglio, of a nonprofit group called Narrative 4, a global story-exchange organization. The group is fronted by writers and artists, including Terry Tempest Williams, Rob Spillman, Greg Khalil, Assaf Gavron, Ishmael Beah, Lila Azam Zanganeh, Tyler Cabot, and several others, including countless numbers of teachers. Our goal is to bring people together to tell one another's stories. *You step into my shoes, I will step into yours.* We see stories and storytelling as the exercise of the ultimate democracy. By dwelling in someone else's story, we believe we can turn empathy into action and help expand the lungs of the world.

In December of 2016, Narrative 4 brought together a group of people from across the United States to share stories under the umbrella of "gun awareness." We gathered police officers, hunters, gun control advocates, victims, gang members, perpetrators, NRA members, and others into the same room in order to see if they might be able to better understand one another. The group included Carolyn Tuft, a mother from Utah who lost her daughter in the Trolley Square mall shootings in 2007. She herself was shot at point-blank range and has so much buckshot in her body that she suffers from lead poisoning. On the other end of the group's spectrum was Todd Underwood, the thirty-seven-year-old owner of United Gun Group, an online gun seller. On his site, Underwood allowed George Zimmerman to auction off the Kel-Tec PF-9 that was used to kill Trayvon Martin. (The pistol went for $250,000, a sum that deserves to be written out—*a quarter of a million dollars* for a weapon that would normally retail for $250.)

Underwood and Tuft were matched up to tell each other's stories. They were about as diametrically opposed in the gun debate as any two people could be: Todd, so deeply for gun ownership, and Carolyn, so personally disturbed by the lack of gun control. When they finally got to tell those stories— "Hi, my name is Carolyn," said Todd, while Carolyn introduced herself as a man who owned 150 guns—the tension in the room was electric. But they managed to make the quantum emotional leap into each other's worlds. For a moment, Todd became Carolyn, and Carolyn became Todd. "For" met "against." Grief met free choice. Shrapnel met flesh. The two began to understand each other differently. They saw with a vision transformed. Something magical occurred in the difficulty of trying to understand a person so completely different. Not so much a chemical reaction as a chimerical one.

Carolyn said that the world had been shifted for her. Her mind hadn't changed about the value of gun ownership, but she understood the complexities of the debate in a far deeper way. A further nuance had crept into her heart. She could feel herself embracing contradiction. It wasn't necessarily comfortable, but it was life altering. Todd too was rocked to the core. He went back to Kansas and immediately began trying to figure out how he could organize story exchanges between Christians and Muslims in his hometown. Most stunning of all is that Todd changed the rules of his online gun website so that visitors to his online message board could no longer use pseudonyms, and purchasers would have to go through an identity check. He and Carolyn became Facebook friends and remain, to this day, in contact with each other.

All of this from looking someone else in the eye. All of this from the simple art of listening and telling.

Our stories, our language, our change.

The late, great Jim Harrison once said that he would rather wear his heart on his sleeve and give full vent to the world of human disappointments than die a smart-ass.

The conviction behind this anthology is that we should be in the habit of hoping and speaking out in favor of that hope. It is, in the end, an optimistic book. The poems assert the possibility of language rather than bullets to open up our veins. To some this may be pure nostalgia. But to others amongst us, we recognize that cynicism is far more nostalgic than any embrace of hope. Cynics live in the sentimental cloud of their own limited territory. They are unable to journey outside of themselves. The optimists are, in fact, the tough and muscular ones. They are ready to place themselves in the line of fire.

What this book can achieve is opening up the grief and the pain to reveal whatever available joy that can be there. This is not a book about the good guys or the bad guys, or even the good guns and the bad guns. It is not a book designed to argue about laws or philosophies or the intricacies of constitutional amendments. Nor is it a book designed by a polemical committee to change your mind.

We can never forget that the good of poetry is first and foremost in the thing itself: the sound, the rhythm, the life-altering order of words. To communicate such suffering beautifully is one of the great paradoxes of the human soul. But it must be done. *How* a poem is said is as vital as *what* it says.

Still, in certain instances poetry has to stand up and shout too. It must kick down the doors and open the windows. It must believe in itself. It must also know that it exists for a reason. Poetry can indeed shift perception. There is a reason we recite poems at funerals and births and weddings. This is where life is most fully engaged. We need a language to celebrate it.

It would be delusional to think that every congressman in this country would suddenly have a change of heart after reading this suite of poems, but it would also be delusional for writers of every color and creed to remain silent. The poetic instinct almost invariably sways toward the just. We have to speak up. Otherwise we are doomed. Silence, as Tahir Djaout says, equates to death. An untold poem would indeed be its own form of suffering.

If you speak, you might just live. So, then, speak and live.

Bullets into Bells

Jordan

NICK ARNOLD

Continue to pour my thoughts out on this topic of discussion
Slow down, I keep gettin the feeling that I'm rushin
Like my cousin's dying breaths, or the decision that was made
But lemme backtrack, letting feelings get in the way
A normal adolescent, aspiring for the highest
Goals that were attainable, wanted to be the flyest
We all searchin for something that we've made a pact to do
The drive of ambition, it's in us, it's in you
Now snatch every dream that a mother had for her son
And replace that with a breath, "Baby, just take another one!"
A white man's gun, the very courier of evil
He left, enjoyed his night, but the gunshots were lethal
Deceitful, everything we've been told from the start
We're more than just some ghetto thugs, these thoughts split us
   apart
What you must understand is our culture bore from oppression
The Hip Hop inside of us a form of expression
I wish I had the chance to explain to Jordan's killer
That the song "Beef" by Lil Reese shouldn't label him a dealer
Or is he ignorant or another ghetto thug?
Do you understand that your ignorance filled him with 3 slugs?
I don't want sympathy and I don't want affection
I want this country to head in the right direction
Instead of discussin who the Grammys should be awardin
Work to prevent murders like those of my cousin, Jordan

Response to "Jordan" from LUCY McBATH,
*Mother of Jordan Davis, National Spokesperson for
Moms Demand Action for Gun Sense in America,
Founder of the Champion in the Making Legacy
Foundation, and a Mother of the Movement*

On the heels of your twenty-second birthday, Jordan, I mourn all of your "firsts" that have been lost since you were murdered four years ago. At times it's hard to stifle my nagging heartache, so I do the only thing that I know to do that feels natural and organic. I cry. I cry for your future that stands incomplete. I cry for the empty spaces that are no longer filled with your laughter. I cry for all the broken dreams and unfulfilled promises that I hold in my hands.

Sometimes I get afraid because I can't feel your presence anymore. I don't want to forget what made you so special. And I don't want to forget the moments when I knew that someday you would be bigger than life itself.

In death, you're still the most important person in my life. And through your beautiful life and death, I will work tirelessly to orchestrate a world that humankind securely lives in without fear and intimidation from gun violence.

Morning Shooting

JIMMY SANTIAGO BACA

4:30
In bed

                        when I hear

an angry voice yell
GO BACK
TO YOUR OWN GODDAMN COUNTRY
DIRTY MEXICAN
wheels screech
a door slams outside
voice begs for mercy
then a scream on the street
and boom! boom!

                        a car squeals off
leaving
a second voice now jagged and weak,
pleading
. . . help. . . .

Did you hear?
Someone's shot! My wife Stacy
rushes from the bedroom to the kitchen,
draws her housecoat on
dashes into the street
and kneels under the streetlight
in the neighbor's driveway

where she lifts the Mexican's
bloody body onto her lap;
blood pools around him
she tugs his arm, he groans
stay awake, stay awake she orders
blood puddles out from his thighs
ladling out surfs
from blown off kneecaps
that look like cantaloupe peelings
on the cutting board.

The shooting takes out the center of me,
leaves pit-molds of two shotgun cartridges
in the center of me smoldering with anger.

This man
was on his way to work
his lunch sack
still clutched in his hand.
As I stare at him
who like all of us journeyed
undocumented
from cosmic
sunlit
regions

into earthling
wombed-being
hands, mouth and lips
breast, ears, toes and hips.

Like all of us
he was all questions—
Mother, what is that and that,
his first sensual exploration into
the world
spark't light-origins
in his heart
that brimmed
sunflower seeds
with brightness,
asking what is that
you said a chili pepper
what is that in the bell tower
you said a pigeon
and in the sand-box
sand between fingers
you said soil
and what is that
feeling your lips on his cheek
you said a kiss
but to him it was happiness
and later as a man
when you ask him
what is that
he hugs you and says love.

I call 911
and ask the police to call the ambulance
but he answers,
He's another gangbanger, let the bitch die

my wife commands him to call
threatens to report him
and he says, the more they kill each other
the better off we are.

After they took the man away,
lawns and bare trees
study the crime scene
to understand what imbues
the dawn with sorrow
darkening it
with the feeling that it's
harder to have hope—
life hits black ice and spins out sometimes,
I tell myself, but that doesn't mean we're lost,
doesn't mean the spinning will never end.

But it does no good,
filled with anger, as I am,
at those who believe in and practice violence,
I drive to the foothills to hike,
where my heart flares its nostrils
quivering leaves
puffing dust,
as pairs of hundred-year-old cedars and piñon trees
root in granite crevices and counsel me in patience.

I have an overwhelming need to cry
for that young man, for me, for us—
so many young Chicanos line the cemetery rows,
so many funeral gatherings daily! I'm sick of it!

How my wife
cradled the man's head in her lap
breathed on his face
it was going to be all right,
her face under the streetlight
smooth as the jade plant
                              in our sunroom,
her voice
wind chimes softly
declaring a belief in peace
and forgiveness.

The man in her arms,
I saw as a school child
cackling racket in shiny hallways
clacking lockers.
He grew wings
his first day at school,
scudded
his chair-desk back
anxious to let his words
fly over
the playground
and perch on the merry-go-round.

His heart's bell hinges grimaced
from so much hard happiness-ringing,
as he raced others
to hopscotch under the shed
or play kickball on the courts,
dangle on monkey bars
and yelp down dented slides.
When I return from my hike
the owners of the house
have already hosed the blood away
a contractor speaks with them
on their plan to install a wall
rimmed with knife blades
to keep intruders from climbing over.

School buses pick up kids
the hour makes its rounds like a jailer
and I feel we are all serving
a sentence for the crime of indifference.

Trump, you declare war
on immigrants and women and children,
all the while the same clichés and rhetoric
spout from your mouth—

What's the promise?
What's the course?
Who prospers?
Who shares in the wealth?
Whose triumph and whose victory?

This day stands in infamy, stands crippled,
stands on blown-off legs,
stands blind and wounded, this day
has no tongue for ordinary Americans,
no ears or hands or jobs or homes,
this day draws the curtain on light,
locks the doors on the needy,
burns books, left our dreams on the barbwire
like a prisoner trying to escape his torturers,
and the biblical prayers,
condemnation of truth,
trashing of gospels—
a day when angels fall from heaven,
a day when wounds open in unborn hearts,
a day when blessings from the lips of pastors
are sins upon us all,
a day of all-out launching of racism,
a day when Christ went into hiding.

The long night begins.

Response to "Morning Shooting" from
ANTONIUS WIRIADJAJA, *Gun Violence*
Survivor (gunsurvivor.antoni.us)

I survived my shooting on the fifth of July, a decade after becoming a naturalized US citizen. I was walking to the subway, and one block from my apartment I heard a loud boom. When I looked down, I saw blood pouring out from my chest. The shooter was aiming for a pregnant woman. I didn't know either of them, but he kept pulling the trigger and one bullet hit me in the chest.

I would have died, but a barber named John D. Morant saw me on the street and placed his hand over mine. I tried to keep in touch, but, less than a year after my shooting, John went away to see family and friends in the South. I called him up and got no answer. A week later, I found out that John had been gunned down and killed.

I'm not the only immigrant who has been shot in the chest. The woman was not the first victim of abuse. And John won't be the last black man shot and killed. You read about us in papers, in poems, and in statistical charts. But we aren't just numbers. We are not words. We are not them. We are people. And I pray that you never become one of us.

I Could Ask,
But I Think They Use Tweezers

AZIZA BARNES

the shoulder is   a complicated organ femoral   artery
lymph   nodes tendons all those joints if a bullet goes

thru you there's also   the clothing   oh yeah what did you
think   I mean if it's just this   then that's different but

if it's   two layers of that   those are other impurities the
body   does its job just one

                function to release what can't stay he walked
into the ER smiled   "I need a doctor   thanks

      man" blood stops moving to the big   towns the
brain is a big town the heart is a big town the kidneys are

            hot spots like Vegas built   to handle
armies on vacation the blood learns   to bend another

way like the legs of a crane   they make bullets
different   now-a-days   in the   good-ole-days

      a bullet went in and out and   the holes
matched now a   .22   a .38   expands in the body

absorbs like a tampon   function   pull in all
life   he was ordering drive thru food   McDonalds

food not   really food maybe like   french fries
maybe like   a Sprite maybe like a #2

                     things that don't feel like food in the
mornings down   the street from my house

      from his mama house a clog   at the 3rd
counter this guy has a gun a gun has   an

operation has composition is orchestral   is an
organ of some complication ephemeral

                the bullets are small a shoulder is
innocuous until you become a nurse the only

                reason he died was speed and
proximity but if it's a couple   layers of cloth well you

have to get that out too

◀ *Response to "I Could Ask, But I Think They Use Tweezers"*
from JUDI RICHARDSON, *Mother of Darien Richardson and*
Founder of Remembering Darien (rememberingdarien.org)

The unimaginable happened to my vibrant and beautiful twenty-five-year-old daughter Darien, her home violently invaded by masked cowards with a gun who shot her several times as she lay sleeping in her own bed. That day was filled with so many conflicting emotions—shock & fear that we would lose her, unbelievable gratitude that she survived, anger that it happened, agonizing empathy & sorrow for all her excruciating pain & suffering, admiration of her strength & courage to endure it all, pride & awe of the way she was handling the ordeal, and so much love for her, happiness & hopefulness that she would recover. Darien was robbed of her normal life, her independence, her ability to sleep peacefully & dance (her favorite), yet she put on a positive air & smiled her beautiful smile & tried to move forward. Little did we know that the damage done by those bullets was too great for her ultimately to survive. I miss her so much; my heart is forever broken, & my soul is shattered. I will never get over this because I shouldn't have to; this should not have happened. This violent homicide is still unsolved, no arrests have been made, the person or persons who did this are still out there. You can get away with murder in this country with a gun. This should concern everyone.

When I Think of Tamir Rice While Driving

REGINALD DWAYNE BETTS

in the backseat of my car are my own sons,
still not yet Tamir's age, already having heard
me warn them against playing with toy pistols,
though my rhetoric is always about what I don't
like, not what I fear, because sometimes
I think of Tamir Rice & shed tears, the weeping
all another insignificance, all another way to avoid
saying what should be said: the Second Amendment
is a ruthless one, the pomp & constitutional circumstance
that says my arms should be heavy with the weight
of a pistol when forced to confront death like
this: a child, a hidden toy gun, an officer that fires
before his heart beats twice. My two young sons play
in the backseat while the video of Tamir dying
plays in my head, & for everything I do know, the thing
I don't say is that this should not be the brick and mortar
of poetry, the moment when a black father drives
his black sons to school & the thing in the air is the death
of a black boy that the father cannot mention,
because to mention the death is to invite discussion
of taboo: if you touch my sons the crimson
that touches the concrete must belong, at some point,
to you, the police officer who justifies the echo
of the fired pistol; taboo: the thing that says that justice

is a killer's body mangled and disrupted by bullets
because his mind would not accept the narrative
of your child's dignity, of his right to life, of his humanity,
and the crystalline brilliance you saw when your boys first
    breathed;
the narrative must invite more than the children bleeding
on crisp fall days; & this is why I hate it all, the people
    around me,
the black people who march, the white people who cheer,
the other brown people, Latinos & Asians & all the colors
    of humanity
that we erase in this American dance around death, as we
are not permitted to articulate the reasons we might yearn
to see a man die; there is so much that has to disappear
for my mind not to abandon sanity: Tamir for instance,
    everything
about him, even as his face, really and truly reminds me
of my own, in the last photo I took before heading off
to a cell, disappears, and all I have stomach for is blood,
and there is a part of me that wishes that it would go away,
the memories, & that I could abandon all talk of making
    it right
& justice. But my mind is no sieve & sanity is no elixir &
    I am bound
to be haunted by the strength that lets Tamir's father,
mother, kinfolk resist the temptation to turn everything
they see into a grave & make home the series of cells
that so many of my brothers already call their tomb.

Response to "When I Think of Tamir Rice While Driving"
from SAMARIA RICE, *Mother of Tamir Rice*

When I think of Tamir as his mother, the woman who gave birth to him, I wonder why my son had to lose his life in such a horrific way in this great place we call America. Police terrorism is real in this country. In many countries this may seem normal, but in America this is not supposed to be normal.

Tamir was an all-American kid with a promising and bright future. Tamir was the life of his family, and I always knew that my son would make some type of change. He was a talented, caring, and loving child. When I lost Tamir, I lost a piece of myself. I was thrown into the political lights and now I am a national leader fighting for human rights.

American police terrorism was created to control the black and brown people of slavery. This remains vivid today. We need change across this country and accountability for our loved ones whose lives have been stolen by American terrorism. Who will govern the government when they continue to murder American citizens? Injustice in this country is pitiful and pathetic. The injustice starts with economics, education, and politicians.

Tamir will always be the reason I continue to do this work and fight for equality of human rights in this country. I am not afraid of the leadership that I have come into upon the death of my son. I am not afraid to create change and to be a part of change.

One Pulse—One Poem

RICHARD BLANCO

*To honor the lives and memory of the victims
of the Pulse tragedy, and to help us all heal.*

Here, sit at my kitchen table, we need to write this
together. Take a sip of *café con leche*, breathe in
the steam and our courage to face this page, bare
as our pain. Curl your fingers around mine, curled
around my pen, hold it like a talisman in our hands
shaking, eyes swollen. But let's not start with tears,
or the flashing lights, the sirens, nor the faint voice
over the cell phone when you heard "I love you . . ."
for the very last time. No, let's ease our way into this,
let our first lines praise the plenitude of morning,
the sun exhaling light into the clouds. Let's imagine
songbirds flocked at my window, hear them chirping
a blessing in Spanish: *bendición-bendición-bendición*

Begin the next stanza with a constant wind trembling
every palm tree, yet steadying our minds just enough
to write out: *bullets, bodies, death*—the vocabulary
of violence raging in our minds, but still mute, choked
in our throats. Leave some white space for a moment
of silence, then fill it with lines repeating the rhythms
pulsing through Pulse that night—salsa, deep house,
electro, merengue, and techno heartbeats mixed with
gunshots. Stop the echoes of that merciless music

with a tender simile to honor the blood of our blood,
without writing *blood*. Use warm words to describe
the cold bodies of our husbands, lovers, and wives,
our sisters, brothers, and friends. Draw a metaphor
so we can picture the choir of their invisible spirits
rising with the smoke toward disco lights, imagine
ourselves dancing with them until the very end.

Write one more stanza—now. Set the page ablaze
with the anger in the hollow ache of our bones—
anger for the new hate, same as the old kind of hate
for the wrong skin color, for the accent in a voice,
for the love of those we're not supposed to love.
Anger for the voice of politics armed with lies, fear
that holds democracy at gunpoint. But let's not
end here. Turn the poem, find details for the love
of the lives lost, still alive in photos—spread them
on the table, give us their wish-filled eyes glowing
over birthday candles, their unfinished sand castles,
their training-wheels, Mickey Mouse ears, tiaras.
Show their blemished yearbook faces, silver-teeth
smiles and stiff prom poses, their tasseled caps
and gowns, their first true loves. And then share
their very last selfies. Let's place each memory
like a star, the light of their past reaching us now,
and always, reminding us to keep writing until
we never need to write a poem like this again.

Response to "One Pulse—One Poem"
from LADD EVERITT, *Director of*
One Pulse for America

Richard Blanco's poem is beautiful. I'll be honest. I've been doing gun violence prevention work for sixteen years. It's hard to acknowledge how precious all these people's lives are while continuing to move forward. Countless men, women, and children are struck down by a weapon that is fetishized and treated like a religious idol in this country. It's almost too much to bear.

My grandfather took his life with a gun. It broke my dad. There was no note. He had to clean up the room. That kind of trauma would tear anybody apart. I don't even want to think about what it feels like to be a parent who loses a child to gun violence. Damn us for allowing this to happen.

I'm in this for the long haul. I'm blessed to be working for George Takei as the director of One Pulse for America (www.1pul.se). There aren't many people who can make some sense of this world we're living in right now. George is one of them.

One day, I hope we can build awe-inspiring memorials to all the beautiful souls we have lost to gun violence and remember them with smiles and laughter. I just wish that day felt closer.

How My Mother Died

TARA BRAY

My father shook the gun to get the bullet out.
He was a careless man, but only once.
I shouldn't linger on this, the road rising out of itself,
my father out on Pine Street in the dark,
down on all fours, trying to open up his face
with gravel, trying to get down to the tar
of what went wrong by making blood again.
They find him there in a dream of twigs
thrashing in the heat, every stitch of light withheld.
Jesus of the ordinary prayer,
lay my father down on a bed of straw
and let him bleed his way to light.
Give him one sweet hour of oblivion,
for all of us. He's out there groveling
in the glare of suspicion, burrowing into the deep
red pit where the lowest sounds are made.
He's borrowed his life from brambles that wait to burn.
I know the dirt won't hide our family,
and the sun's intensity won't take root in the sky,
make truth a thing we all can see.
So let my father drift away from here
holding your brown feet.
Stir your crown of glory into his bleary eyes and sing
the untroubled prayer, the warm treason of innocence.
Ready us both for the undoing,
that can't, for the life of him, be undone.

Response to "How My Mother Died" from
Dennis Henigan, *Author of* "Guns Don't Kill
People, People Kill People" and Other Myths
About Guns and Gun Control

I respond to this provocative poem as a long-time and non-violent combatant in the deeply emotional national debate over gun violence. For me, "How My Mother Died" communicates three grim realities about gun violence.

First, few tragedies can befall a family that are as sudden, and as instantly transforming, as a shooting. A gunshot changes everything in a moment, while inflicting pain that lasts a lifetime for all involved. For me, this poem is about that pain.

Second, in so many shootings, the person who suffered the wound is not the only victim. The poem is about the shooting of the poet's mother, but her father—who apparently was handling the gun—was also a victim. It is his pain that is shared through these powerful words. Two victims—and victims of what? Victims of the gun.

Third, guns are unforgiving. A single mistake in an ordinary moment with a gun ("He was a careless man, but only once."), and a life ends, with no prospect of absolution. For the occasionally careless, or the temporarily suicidal, or the sometimes hot-tempered, guns afford no second chances. Guns make the lethal difference. Guns do, indeed, kill people.

Bullet Points

JERICHO BROWN

I will not shoot myself
In the head, and I will not shoot myself
In the back, and I will not hang myself
With a trashbag, and if I do
I promise you, I will not do it
In a police car while handcuffed
Or in the jail cell of a town
I only know the name of
Because I have to drive through it
To get home. Yes, I may be at risk,
But I promise you, I trust the maggots
And the ants and the roaches
Who live beneath the floorboards
Of my house to do what they must
To any carcass more than I trust
An officer of the law of the land
To shut my eyes like a man
Of God might, or to cover me with a sheet
So clean my mother could have used it
To tuck me in. When I kill me, I will kill me
The same way most Americans do,
I promise you: cigarette smoke
Or a piece of meat on which I choke
Or so broke I freeze
In one of these winters we keep

Calling worst. I promise that if you hear
Of me dead anywhere near
A cop, then that cop killed me. He took
Me from us and left my body, which is,
No matter what we've been taught,
Greater than the settlement a city can
Pay to a mother to stop crying, and more
Beautiful than the brand new shiny bullet
Fished from the folds of my brain

Michael Skolnik, *Entrepreneur and Activist*

I was taught as a young boy that the police were my friends, that their job was to protect me and to serve my community, that the police captured the "bad guys" and put them in jail. I waved hello to them when I saw them in my town. I smiled at them in the local diner sipping coffee on an early morning before school began. I had nothing to fear when I was pulled over a few times after I learned how to drive. When they approached my car, I didn't fear their gun; I feared a piece of paper with a fine that would cost me a few extra bucks. But I never feared for my life. I was just another white kid growing up in a country that gave me the benefit of the doubt, every single time. Privilege. White privilege.

Mr. Brown's "Bullet Points" gives me stomachaches. It hurts my head. It pains my soul. The fact that so many people of color in this country have good reason to fear for their lives during encounters with law enforcement is one of the greatest promises of freedom that we, the United States of America, have broken over the course of our nation's history. The fix to that broken promise will not be found in the "bad seed" theory. Rather, we must fix an entire system that is propped up by the fear and interrogation of a group of people who pose no greater threat to society than us white people. Let this magnificently powerful poem inspire us to do the work to put an end to our children living different realities of freedom because of their skin color.

22

BRIAN CLEMENTS

The guy my girlfriend ran off with
in 1983 drove a rusted-out Beetle
and carried a .22 pistol for runs to the bank
to drop off nightly deposits from the General
Cinema, where he was Assistant Manager
and where I worked and saw Rocky Horror
about 20 times more than I wanted to
in egg-and-tp-drenched midnight shows.
He lived in a rat-trap, roach-infested, leaning-over
shack on the edge of The Heights,
a few streets over from the house where,
in 2004, a local TV reporter was murdered
in her bed, her face beaten beyond recognition.

—

In 1988, on my first night as Assistant Manager
at a restaurant in Dallas, a fight broke out
between a pimp and a private investigator,
who also may have been a pimp. A group
of frat boys decided to jump in and knocked
the whole scrum over onto the floor
just on the other side of the bar from me.
The pimp came up pointing a .22 semiautomatic
directly at the closest object, which happened
to be my forehead. He didn't shoot—
just waved his gun around until everyone
cowered under their tables—then
calmly walked out the front door and down the street.

—

My best friend in sixth or seventh grade
moved to Arkansas from New Mexico.
Ron's skin was lizard-rough.
He raised hamsters and hermit crabs.
I struck him out for the last out of the Little League
Championship. We went out to his father's farm
and shot cans and bottles with his .22 rifle.
Back in New Mexico, he'd had some health problems
and his mother had shot herself in the head.
A few years ago, a dead body was found
buried on his father's property. Ron's son
ended up shooting himself in the head as well.
He was 22.

—

On December 14, 2012, an armed gunman
entered the Sandy Hook School with two pistols,
a Bushmaster .223, hundreds of rounds of ammunition,
and a shotgun in the car. Rather than turn right,
toward my wife's classroom where she pulled
two kids into her room from the hallway,
he turned to the left, murdered twenty children
and six adults, including the principal
and the school psychologist, both of whom
went into the hallway to stop the gunman,
and shot two other teachers, who survived.
After that, a lot of other things happened,
but it doesn't really matter what.

◀ *Response to "22" from* Po KIM MURRAY,
Cofounder of Newtown Action Alliance

It did not matter to the National Rifle Association (NRA), the Republican members of Congress, Donald Trump, Republican governors, Republican state legislators, and some Democratic leaders that my neighbor killed his mother in her bed, then drove to Sandy Hook Elementary School to brutally gun down twenty children and six educators with an AR-15 with high-capacity magazines, *or* that a hundred thousand Americans are killed or injured by guns in our towns and cities across the nation every single year, *or* that there are nearly three hundred mass shooting incidents annually.

It mattered to us. We are a group of Newtown, Connecticut, neighbors and friends who formed the Newtown Action Alliance, a grassroots group advocating for cultural and legislative changes to end gun violence in our nation.

It mattered to 90 percent of Americans who support expanded background checks.

It mattered to families of victims and survivors directly impacted by gun violence.

Because it still matters to us, we will work to hold all state and federal elected representatives accountable for standing with the NRA instead of taking action to keep all of us safe from gun violence.

Despite the NRA rhetoric, we know firsthand that guns kill and guns don't make us safer.

Boy Shooting at a Statue

BILLY COLLINS

It was late in the afternoon,
the beginning of winter, a light snow,
and I was the only one in the small park

to witness the boy running alone
in circles around the base of a bronze statue.
I could not read the carved name

of the noted statesmen
who loomed above, one hand on a cold hip,
the other thrust into his frozen waistcoat.

And the boy had only his hand for a gun,
but as he ran, head down,
he would lift a finger to the statue

pulling an imaginary trigger
as he imitated the sounds of rapid fire.
Evening thickened, the mercury sank,

but the boy kept running in the circle
of his own footprints in the snow
as he shot blindly into the air.

History will never find a way to end,
I thought, as I left the park by the north gate
and returned to the station of my desk

where the sheets of paper I wrote on
served as pieces of glass, through which I could see
swarms of dark birds circling in the sky below.

Response to "Boy Shooting at a Statue" from
NICOLE HOCKLEY, *Mother of Dylan Hockley,*
Cofounder of Dylan's Wings of Change, and
Managing Director of Sandy Hook Promise

The issue of gun violence is one of the most polarized and divisive topics in our nation. Misinformation and rhetoric from all sides sustain the endless cycle of conflict, limiting even small advances. It's not a conversation seeking common ground, or one in which anyone considers compromise acceptable, even though the universal goal is so simple: saving lives.

So who is responsible for delivering the changes we need to prevent further violence, injury, and death? Is it the gun manufacturer? The purchaser? Is it the boy holding the gun? Is it the frozen statesman who allows the cycle to continue? Or is it the bystander, passively observing but not acting?

I believe it is all of the above, as well as all of us, the readers, who are responsible. One man murdered my son, but so many others took no action to intervene in the shooter's destructive life or to prevent his easy access to firearms. My beautiful boy's murder could have been prevented.

For the rest of my life I will work to create that conversation, find that common ground, and save the lives of others. We must end this long winter and break the current cycle of history to find a new path to the future, where all children are safe.

Natural Causes

KYLE DARGAN

Naturally, the gun is purchased from a farm in Virginia—
pulled from a bushel of barrels by a tremulous hand, a young
man's. His other fist proffers sweat-wilted dollars. The farmer,
compensated, keeps his gaze down so as to remember nothing
of the boy's face. A young face is another young face. His
customers rarely return older. Seasons matter little to him—
none of the guns he sells are grown from seed. Each a plug he
only tends until maturity, harvest. Naturally, he will not smell
the fused aroma of sulfur, and specters escaping the bodies
of the boys this boy will smoke upwind, upriver. In D.C. In
Prince George's. Leaves burn where the farmer lives. Deer and
turkeys hunted, but never with the pistols he sells to these
boys who trade fire with boys. Many of them will not live to
see any creature of the woods, though their dumped corpses
may share the woods with the deer and the turkeys. And the
leaves. Every year the leaves bury memory of those juvenile
graves—the crackling umbers and rusts muting to umbrage
what otherwise should be rage.

Response to "Natural Causes" from
DANIEL WEBSTER, *Professor and*
Director of the Johns Hopkins Center
for Gun Policy and Research

Guns often mean different things to Americans living in rural areas than to people living in areas of concentrated and institutionalized urban poverty. Kyle Dargan's "Natural Causes" reveals the connections between these worlds through the eyes of a farmer who does not want to consider the natural and deadly consequences of his sales of guns to youths. The absence of background checks and sales records means these sales entail little risk to sellers. My studies have shown consistent connections between policies that require gun-seller accountability and fewer guns being diverted for criminal use. Gun tracing enables police to investigate how guns make their way to teenagers and violent criminals. These investigations usually occur when a police officer is shot or gun violence invades a community assumed to be safe from gun violence. Yet, when men sell guns in ways that predictably lead to deaths of black boys and men, our laws and enforcement too rarely render justice. Most gun owners want stronger measures to hold scofflaw gun sellers accountable. Give them what they want.

Wednesday Poem

JOEL DIAS-PORTER

Ta-Nehisi and I pass through the metal detector
inside the front doors of Cardozo High
with xeroxed poems and a lesson planned
to introduce our students to the Wild Iris.
After signing our names in the visitor's log,
we bop down two flights of steps.
Outside the classroom things are too quiet
and why does Mr. Bruno (who's Boriqua and writes poetry)
take ten minutes to answer the door?
There's a student snapshot in his hand.
One of our kids got shot last night,
Remember Maurice?, Maurice Caldwell.
He didn't come to school much.
A Crisis Response Team has the kids in a circle
and have we ever seen them sit so quietly?
Every computer in the classroom is dead.
A drawing of Maurice is taped to the board,
a bouquet of cards pinned under it,
Keisha (who writes funny poems in class)
says Maurice would help her with Math,
she liked him but never told him.
The Crisis lady says *It's OK to cry.*
Keisha says she been ran out of tears.
Mr. Bruno tells me *Somebody called him*
from a parked Buick on Thomas Place NW.

When he walked up, they fired three times.
I freeze. That's a half block from my house.
There are four crackhouses on that block
and I never walk down that street.
Why did he approach the car,
was he hustling crack or weed?
Did he recognize the dude and smile
before surprise blossomed across his face
and the truth rooted into his flesh?
His face flashes before my irises,
he's horseplaying with Haneef,
his hair slicked back into a ponytail.
He wrote one poem this whole semester,
a battle rap between cartoon characters.
Mr. Bruno asks if we still want to teach.
I open my folder of nature poems,
then close the folder, and slump in a chair.
Which student could these pistils protect,
here where it's natural to never see seventeen?

Response to "Wednesday Poem" from
Kiki Leyba, *Columbine High School Teacher*

I enter through the doors you watched students flee from like
Defectors.
There is no lesson
plan for death and tragedy.
I'll never hear anything louder than guns in here.
Eighteen years
I leave a prayer outside
Columbine, Sandy Hook, Marysville-Pilchuk
Virginia Tech, Umpqua, Arapahoe;
I've been a visitor in a log
in circles searching eyes
wishing truths were distant lies,
saying things my children don't know.
I hid
under a desk, bottom of glass,
front of class, time alone,
writing where death and resurrection
had no nail wood connection.

6:00 a.m.
Do students recognize all of
THIS
upon my face?

Do my eyes flash fear
when we hear the alarm to clear
The Building?
I want them to see all of me.
The darkest days grow strength
in ways I don't want to learn or speak of.
To let the lessons sit in me
a *soul unable to speak*
is a fool's choice.
I've returned from *oblivion*.
Could other victims grow?
Buds of darkness become the flowers of night
if I share my story, give it voice,
if they can reach out and ask to speak
about this thing so unnatural to speak aloud.

Catching Copper

NATALIE DIAZ

My brothers have
a bullet.

They keep their bullet
on a leash shiny
as a whip of blood.

My brothers walk their bullet
with a limp—a clipped
hip bone.

My brothers' bullet
is a math-head, is all geometry,
from a distance is just a bee
and its sting. Like a bee—
you should see my brothers' bullet
make a comb, by chewing holes
in what is sweet.

My brothers lose
their bullet all the time—
when their bullet takes off on them,
their bullet leaves a hole.

My brothers search their houses,
their bodies for their bullet,
and a little red ghost moans.

Eventually, my brothers call out,
Here, bullet, here—
their bullet comes running, buzzing.
Their bullet always comes
back to them. When their bullet comes
back to them, their bullet
leaves a hole.

My brothers are too slow
for their bullet
because their bullet is in a hurry
and wants to get the lead out.

My brothers' bullet is dressed
for a red carpet
in a copper jacket.

My brothers tell their bullet,
Careful you don't hurt somebody
with all that flash.

My brothers kiss their bullet
in a dark cul-de-sac, in front
of the corner store ice machine,
in the passenger seat of their car,
on a strobe-lighted dance floor.
My brothers' bullet
kisses them back.

My brothers break and dance
for their bullet—the jerk,
the stanky leg. They pop, lock
and drop for their bullet,
a move that has them writhing
on the ground—
the worm, my brothers call it.
Yes, my brothers go all-worm
for their bullet.

My brothers' bullet is registered,
is a bullet of letters—has a PD,
a CIB, a GSW, if they are lucky
an EMT, if not, a Triple 9, a DNR,
a DOA.

My brothers never call the cops
on their bullet and instead pledge
allegiance to their bullet
with hands over their hearts
and stomachs and throats.

My brothers say they would die
for their bullet. If my brothers die,
their bullet would be lost.
If my brothers die,
there's no bullet to begin with—
the bullet is for living brothers.

My brothers feed their bullet
the way the bulls fed Zeus—
burning, on a pyre, their own
thigh bones wrapped in fat.
My brothers take a knee, bow
against the asphalt, prostrate
on the concrete for their bullet.

We wouldn't go so far
as to call our bullet
a prophet, my brothers say.
But my brothers' bullet
is always lit like a night-church.
It makes my brothers holy.
You could say my brothers' bullet
cleans them—the way red ants
wash the empty white bowl
of a dead coyote's eye socket.
Yes, my brothers' bullet
cleans them, makes them
ready for god.

Response to "Catching Copper" from
THE REVEREND HENRY BROWN,
Founder of Mothers United Against Violence

I am a survivor of gun violence, but I wasn't the first in my family affected. I lost a brother who was sixteen at the time of his death; he was killed in a hunting accident. Then, sixteen years later, on the first day I was discharged from the military, I was shot once in the chest and was in a coma for three weeks. Every dream I had of becoming a professional baseball player died on that fateful night.

In 2001, gun violence was reintroduced into my life in Hartford, Connecticut, when a seven-year-old child was shot in the face. It was that incident, not my own encounter with gun violence, that compelled me to action on behalf of all people affected by this epidemic. Since that day I have served as a voice for people impacted by violence, especially in Hartford, where gun violence is a daily occurrence.

In my many years in this fight, I have seen a lack of concern for gun violence in urban and poor neighborhoods, particularly when it happens to people of color. This is a grave injustice. I have seen men, women, and children shot dead or wounded in their homes, and still the bullets fly. I have held hundreds of prayer vigils and antiviolence rallies, and still the bullets fly. I often wonder, if this injustice were occurring in suburban communities would the bullets be allowed to fly. Maybe if more of us showed we cared, then maybe the guns would be silent, and the bullets would fly no more.

In Two Seconds

MARK DOTY

Tamir Rice, 2002–2014

the boy's face
climbed back down the twelve-year tunnel

of its becoming, a charcoal sunflower
swallowing itself. Who has eyes to see,

or ears to hear? If you could see
what happens fastest, unmaking

the human irreplaceable, a star
falling into complete gravitational

darkness from all points of itself, all this:

the held loved body into which entered
milk and music, honeying the cells of him:

who sang to him, stroked the nap
of the scalp, kissed the flesh-knot

after the cord completed its work
of fueling into him the long history

of those whose suffering
was made more bearable

by the as-yet-unknown of him,

playing alone in some unthinkable
future city, a Cleveland,

whatever that might be.
Two seconds. To elapse:

the arc of joy in the conception bed,
the labor of hands repeated until

the hands no longer required attention,
so that as the woman folded

her hopes for him sank into the fabric
of his shirts and underpants. Down

they go, swirling down into the maw
of a greater dark. Treasure box,

comic books, pocket knife, bell from a lost cat's collar,
why even begin to enumerate them

when behind every tributary
poured into him comes rushing backward

all he hasn't been yet. Everything
that boy could have thought or made,

sung or theorized, built on the quavering
but continuous structure

that had preceded him sank into
an absence in the shape of a boy

playing with a plastic gun in a city park
in Ohio, in the middle of the afternoon.

When I say two seconds, I don't mean the time
it took him to die. I mean the lapse between

the instant the cruiser braked to a halt
on the grass, between that moment

and the one in which the officer fired his weapon.
The two seconds taken to *assess the situation*.

And though I believe it is the work
of art to try on at least the moment
and skin of another,

for this hour I respectfully decline.

I refuse it. May that officer
be visited every night of his life
by an enormity collapsing in front of him

into an incomprehensible bloom,
and the voice that howls out of it.

If this is no poem then . . .

But that voice—erased boy,
beloved of time, who did nothing
to no one and became

nothing because of it—I know that voice
is one of the things we call poetry.
It isn't to his killer he's speaking.

Response to "In Two Seconds" from
PASTOR MICHAEL MCBRIDE, *Director of*
Urban Strategies and Live Free Campaign for
the PICO (People Improving Communities
Through Organizing) National Network

God has no pleasure in the death of anyone, says the ancient prophet, but that all would turn and live. And yet this divine declaration seems to be outpaced by our death-dealing culture.

Our addiction to lethal violence, largely through guns, sentences both the young and the old, the citizen and the police officer, the colonizer and the colonized to a most terrible fate of both executioner and executed.

Since death does not please our Creator, surely life unleashes an abundant and healing joy, infusing creation with peace.

This must be our work in the days ahead.

Unleashing Joy. Making Peace. Healing Trauma.

Not to do so renders our life susceptible to practices that leave both God and Creation groaning for a world not intended.

A violent world unable to be sustained.

May our words *and* actions reflect a commitment to repent from this death-dealing way of life, to defeat what Dr. Martin Luther King called the triplets of evil: racism, militarism, and economic exploitation.

Only in this way will the lives lost and the lives left to steward be worthy of a future not yet realized but surely intended: a pleased Creator and a peaceful creation.

Meditation at Fifty Yards, Moving Target

RITA DOVE

Safety First.

Never point your weapon, keep your finger
off the trigger. Assume a loaded barrel,
even when it isn't, especially when you *know* it isn't.
Glocks are lightweight but sensitive;
the Keltec has a long pull and a kick.
Rifles have penetrating power, viz.:
if the projectile doesn't lodge in its mark,
it will travel some distance
until it finds shelter; it will certainly
pierce your ordinary drywall partition.
You could wound the burglar and kill your child
sleeping in the next room, all with one shot.

Open Air.

Fear, of course. Then the sudden
pleasure of heft—as if the hand
had always yearned for this solemn
fit, this *gravitas*, and now had found
its true repose.

Don't pull the trigger, squeeze it—
squeeze between heartbeats.

Look down the sights. Don't
hold your breath. Don't hold
anything, just stop breathing.
Level the scene with your eyes. Listen.
Soft, now: squeeze.

Gender Politics.

Guys like noise: rapid fire,
thunk-and-slide of a blunt-nose silver Mossberg,
or double-handed Colts, slugging it out from the hips.
Rambo or cowboy, they'll whoop it up.

Women are fewer, more elegant.
They prefer precision:
tin cans swing-dancing in the trees,
the paper bull's-eye's tidy rupture at fifty yards.

> (Question: If you were being pursued,
>   how would you prefer to go down—
>   ripped through a blanket of fire
>   or plucked by one incandescent
>   fingertip?)

The Bullet.

dark dark no wind no heaven
i am not anything   not borne on air   i bear
myself   i can slice the air   no wind
can hold me   let me   let me
go   i can see   yes

o aperture o light   let me   off
go off   straight is my verb   straight
my glory road   yes   now i can   feel
it the light i am flame   velocity o
beautiful body i am coming i am yours
before you know it
i am home

◄ Response to "Meditation at Fifty Yards, Moving Target"
from MARIE DELUS, *Marine Veteran, Sharpshooter, and*
Moms Demand Action for Gun Sense in America Activist

As a female sharpshooter, I remember the first time I lifted a rifle and the joy I felt when I hit my first bull's-eye after the first shot; I hit it again and again. Everyone around me was impressed and surprised. I wasn't the type, didn't fit their notion of what a sharpshooter looks like.

Many years later, I lost a nephew not by a rifle but a gun. It has been years since I shot a rifle, yet I remember the joy, the accomplishment. Now the memory is clouded with guilt that I myself am trained in the use of weapons for killing in war and that my nephew was shot to death.

In Newtown, on December 14, 2012, twenty innocent babies died and six heroic educators.

I am often asked as a former Marine—a sharpshooter—what is the difference?

Twenty-six innocent people died because of a weapon meant to kill.

Twenty were children, and they will never enjoy their first crush or heartbreak, achieve their first A in school, defy their parents, have their first graduation and prom, get a job, walk down the aisle at their wedding, have a baby, become a grandparent, die a natural death.

What is the difference? For me, if you have to ask what is the difference between children dying in their school and soldiers dying in war, then we have another battle entirely on our hands.

Gun Poem

CORNELIUS EADY

Look, I hate guns,
But I remember that afternoon
My big sister, Gloria
Came to visit us in
New York, with her
Pistol in her purse,

And thinking, what if;
The poor son of a bitch
Crook, thinking he read
It right, but only as far
As myself and my wife
The kind of people

Who give it up, and misreading
My sister, probably smiling,
Opening her purse like
Pandora. I remember
Thinking, as we walked
Unharmed to wherever,

The cartoon widening
Of the perp's eyes
As he drank it in,
Oops, leveling
And drawing a bead
Towards his ass-hole face.

In a fight, my sister told me
Two things: get them down
And keep them down.
With a gun, hit the head,
Be certain. This is what
Childhood taught her.

You'll be sorry, she never said
That day you turn the wrong corner,
Float against the wrong crew.
In the fist and fury, you'll long
For what you say you don't need,
This spell I carry against
The real.

◀ *Response to "Gun Poem" from*
RONNIE MOSLEY, *Generation Progress*
Gun Violence Prevention Organizer

For many of us, making the decision to take action on gun violence is a matter of perspective. Do we see ourselves as safe or in danger?

Our nation is better than accepting the fear of turning the wrong corner because we choose not to address the source of our fear of what's around the corner.

For me, fears have been made reality far too often. My name comes from a cousin who was shot and killed blocks away from home. My great-grandmother was shot on her front porch in a drive-by. My friend Blair died shielding a friend on a city bus leaving his high school. My uncle is confined to a wheelchair from being shot. Still, I choose not to own a gun because I can say with confidence that owning a gun would not have changed any of that. I choose to try to change the way people think—to stop people from wanting to pick up guns in the first place before using them to act irrationally. The best way to honor the lives of those I lost is to prevent it from happening again.

There always is a choice one can make.

Heal the Cracks in the Bell of the World

MARTÍN ESPADA

For the community of Newtown, Connecticut,
where twenty students and six educators lost their
lives to a gunman at Sandy Hook Elementary School,
December 14, 2012

Now the bells speak with their tongues of bronze.
Now the bells open their mouths of bronze to say:
Listen to the bells a world away. Listen to the bell in the ruins
of a city where children gathered copper shells like beach glass,
and the copper boiled in the foundry, and the bell born
in the foundry says: *I was born of bullets, but now I sing*
of a world where bullets melt into bells. Listen to the bell
in a city where cannons from the armies of the Great War
sank into molten metal bubbling like a vat of chocolate,
and the many mouths that once spoke the tongue of smoke
form the one mouth of a bell that says: *I was born of cannons,*
but now I sing of a world where cannons melt into bells.

Listen to the bells in a town with a flagpole on Main Street,
a rooster weathervane keeping watch atop the Meeting House,
the congregation gathering to sing in times of great silence.
Here the bells rock their heads of bronze as if to say:
Melt the bullets into bells, melt the bullets into bells.
Here the bells raise their heavy heads as if to say:
Melt the cannons into bells, melt the cannons into bells.

Here the bells sing of a world where weapons crumble deep
in the earth, and no one remembers where they were buried.
Now the bells pass the word at midnight in the ancient language
of bronze, from bell to bell, like ships smuggling news of liberation
from island to island, the song rippling through the clouds.

Now the bells chime like the muscle beating in every chest,
heal the cracks in the bell of every face listening to the bells.
The chimes heal the cracks in the bell of the moon.
The chimes heal the cracks in the bell of the world.

Response to "Heal the Cracks in the Bell of the World"
from DAVID AND FRANCINE WHEELER, *Parents of*
Ben Wheeler and Founders of Ben's Lighthouse

In the period following the murder of our son, this poem was read at several gatherings and at one, I, David, spoke the words myself. We feel the irony of the location of our loss: Connecticut, the birthplace of the American firearms industry: Newtown, the home of that industry's trade group. Nearby Waterbury, the former brass foundry capital of the country, where furnaces melted brass to make bells, shifting their production to shell casings for the war effort. New Haven, home of Eli Whitney, who advanced the mass production of firearms more than anyone. To move through this landscape, day after day, carrying the weight of our murdered boy in the hole in our hearts just his shape and size, is an unwanted permanent texture of our lives. It is, however, eclipsed in dimension by the support, assistance, and love of our community tucked in these same hills, a community where we work to support, teach, and help others through the organization Ben's Lighthouse, created to honor Ben, his classmates, and his teachers, working to heal wherever we can. Helping is Healing.

So we stay and we listen for the bells.

Aubade with Lemon and Sage

TARFIA FAIZULLAH

First I said, yes, here
by the light. The dark
has its own blindfold,
the pearls of the eyes
of anyone who will leave
you—sprig of sage

for your hair, he said.
Rind of lemon for
your fingers, and la
ilaha illallah I whistled,
though the dawn eats
its own faith, rubs aromatics

into the question of what
comes after the next air raid
or bombing or shooting
and the morning is blank
and the sun shines down
on another blatant river

of limbs. First I said,
tomorrow, then, now,
I'll leave now, while
it's still safe. A few
more minutes, love,
he said, a few more

hours. Just trust,
he said. I said yes
to the sprig of sage
and the rind of lemon
until the uniformed man
smiled and raised his gun

higher towards the sound
a human body makes
when it's about to fly.
I made no sound
but the sound a wraith
makes as it starves

itself goodbye.
I said sprig, said rind—
and watched him die.
First I begged, grave.
Then I said, above.
and lifted what was

left of my wing higher.

◀ *Response to "Aubade with Lemon and Sage"*
from SHARBARI AHMED,
author of The Ocean of Ms. Nagai
and Former Writer for ABC's Quantico

Lemon and sage. I imagine the Holey Artisan Bakery in Dhaka smelled of lemon and sage one July afternoon when twelve young men, brandishing guns and machetes, walked in and proceeded to shoot and or hack to death twenty-two people. They said my friend, Ishrat, was defiant. They said when she was asked to recite the Koran, she refused, saying she didn't have to prove her fealty to her faith. They said the young men, wearing the uniforms of ISIS—headscarves and perverse righteousness—smiled and raised their guns and knives and murdered her.

Where did these children get these guns? Perhaps they were so brainwashed, even if they didn't have guns they would have made weapons of whatever they could find. The reality is that somehow gun violence has been glorified. This is one of the ways groups like ISIS recruit their "martyrs." I see this everywhere, however. In Hollywood, an influential arbiter of public sentiment, violence with guns is couched as macho. A svelte young woman brandishing a gun is somehow rendered powerful and sexy. In a world where so many feel powerless and small, a gun is a talisman against insignificance. This may be our undoing.

A Poem for Pulse

JAMESON FITZPATRICK

Last night, I went to a gay bar
with a man I love a little.
After dinner, we had a drink.
We sat in the far-back of the big backyard
and he asked, What will we do when this place closes?
I don't think it's going anywhere any time soon, I said,
though the crowd was slow for a Saturday,
and he said—Yes, but one day. Where will we go?
He walked me the half-block home
and kissed me goodnight on my stoop—
properly: not too quick, close enough
our stomachs pressed together
in a second sort of kiss.
I live next to a bar that's not a gay bar
—we just call those bars, I guess—
and because it is popular
and because I live on a busy street,
there are always people who aren't queer people
on the sidewalk on weekend nights.
Just people, I guess.
They were there last night.
As I kissed this man I was aware of them watching
and of myself wondering whether or not they were just.
But I didn't let myself feel scared, I kissed him
exactly as I wanted to, as I would have without an audience,
because I decided many years ago to refuse this fear—

an act of resistance. I left
the idea of hate out on the stoop and went inside,
to sleep, early and drunk and happy.
While I slept, a man went to a gay club
with two guns and killed forty-nine people.
Today in an interview, his father said he had been disturbed
recently by the sight of two men kissing.
What a strange power to be cursed with:
for the proof of men's desire to move men to violence.
What's a single kiss? I've had kisses
no one has ever known about, so many
kisses without consequence—
but there is a place you can't outrun,
whoever you are.
There will be a time when.
It might be a bullet, suddenly.
The sound of it. Many.
One man, two guns, fifty dead—
Two men kissing. Last night
I can't get away from, imagining it, them,
the people there to dance and laugh and drink,
who didn't believe they'd die, who couldn't have.
How else can you have a good time?
How else can you live?
There must have been two men kissing
for the first time last night, and for the last,
and two women, too, and two people who were neither.
Brown people, which cannot be a coincidence in this country
which is a racist country, which is gun country.
Today I'm thinking of the Bernie Boston photograph

Flower Power, of the Vietnam protestor placing carnations
in the rifles of the National Guard,
and wishing for a gesture as queer and simple.
The protester in the photo was gay, you know,
he went by Hibiscus and died of AIDS,
which I am also thinking about today because
(the government's response to) AIDS was a hate crime.
Now we have a president who names us,
the big and imperfectly lettered us, and here we are
getting kissed on stoops, getting married some of us,
some of us getting killed.
We must love one another whether or not we die.
Love can't block a bullet
but neither can it be shot down,
and love is, for the most part, what makes us—
in Orlando and in Brooklyn and in Kabul.
We will be everywhere, always;
there's nowhere else for us, or you, to go.
Anywhere you run in this world, love will be there to greet you.
Around any corner, there might be two men. Kissing.

Response to "A Poem for Pulse" from KEVIN
HERTZOG, *Gays Against Guns Cofounder and Activist*

In 1982, I'd been living in New York City for two months,
and I'd been wanting to find camaraderie and companion-
ship, but I had no idea how to find them. Finally, one eve-
ning, I sniffed out an establishment from which I'd noticed
handsome young men coming and going.

Nightclubs were safe spaces where my "family of choice"
assembled. They were places where being gay or gender-
nonconforming or trans or just plain weird got transformed
from being liabilities into being currency. In nightclubs, I
learned how to live.

Omar Mateen's shooting spree radicalized me. I was con-
sumed with despair for the people mown down before their
lives had really started. And it wasn't only the fact that they
died so young, but it was also that they'd died at a gay club.
They went there to be with "their people." And they were
ruthlessly murdered, because an unhinged man had previ-
ously witnessed two men kissing and couldn't deal with his
complicated feelings about that kiss.

The people who died in that nightclub deserve an advo-
cate. They deserve to have a voice. I decided that I would try
to be that voice. So I met up with like-minded folks, many
of whom had also spent substantial time in gay nightclubs,
and we formed Gays Against Guns, an inclusive group of
LGBTQ people and their allies who are committed to non-
violently breaking the gun industry's chain of death.

My Mother Contemplating Her Gun

NICK FLYNN

One boyfriend said to keep the bullets

locked in a different room.
                        Another urged
        clean it
or it could explode. Larry

thought I should keep it loaded
under my bed,
            you never know.

        I bought it
when I didn't feel safe. The barrel
            is oily,

        reflective, the steel

pure, pulled from a hole
                in West Virginia. It

could have been cast into anything, nails
along the carpenter's lip, the ladder

to balance the train. Look at this, one
      bullet,

      how almost nothing it is—

saltpeter sulphur lead Hell

burns sulphur, a smell like this.
      safety & hammer, barrel & grip

      I don't know what I believe.

I remember the woods behind my father's house
      horses beside the quarry

stolen cars lost in the deepest wells,
the water below
      an ink waiting to fill me.

      Outside a towel hangs from a cold line
a sheet of iron in the sky

roses painted on it, blue roses.

Tomorrow it will still be there.

Response to "My Mother Contemplating Her Gun"
from ASHLYN MELTON, *Bereaved Mother of*
Noah James Daigle (6/18/98–12/30/11)

Life is precious. God decided when we would be born. Unfortunately, sometimes man decides when we will die.

My son, Noah Daigle, had a purpose in life. He was an absolute joy and was destined for great things. No worries at the tender age of thirteen. But in one second, a dumb decision destroyed his life and the lives of all of us who are left on earth to grieve. One irresponsible, not-thought-out action by a child ended Noah's life December 30, 2011. Others refer to it as an accident. Don't call it an accident. That undermines all I try to do in sharing his story. It was a negligent incident. It was free will. It was a choice made by his friend. A choice to pick up an unsecured, unlocked gun. A choice that will stay with me all the rest of my days.

The Brady Campaign to Prevent Gun Violence quickly realized that these types of tragic deaths were happening too frequently. It seemed normal for children to lose their lives this way, and they wanted to do something about that. They started ASK (Asking Saves Kids) Day, which is June 21st of each year. The purpose is to encourage people to ask about guns and gun storage in every home your child visits. ASK and then you make the choice if you think your child will be safe in that home. Don't do what I did. Don't be naive in thinking your child is being watched the way that you would watch them. The reality is they are not always safe. I didn't ASK and now I visit my child at the graveyard.

Gunning for It

REBECCA MORGAN FRANK

Have you ever smelled the residue? Surely
a car has backfired on your street, sent your
pulse climbing up the back stairs. Have you
ever held the cold power in your palm? Heats
up from your body, doesn't it? Cools down
the body it hits. Have you seen the warmth
wiped out of skin? When you haven't you know
the numbers are gunning for you. They'll track
you down anywhere with ease. Violence rests
everywhere, even in your histories. Take me,
for example: an ancestor shot a man in the head
once—he stopped a mass murderer
in his tracks. How do you explain a history
like that? By telling the whole story? How
the relative also left another man for dead,
having hit him over the head with rage?
He had that kind of temper. The innocent
man happened to live, just as the guilty man
fell dead before he took a street of lives.
Justice just an accident where violence
meets its match, lucks into the history of merit.
You touch the gun, it breathes in, breathes out.
Plots a future of its own, weighs its chances
of righteousness, of the right hand unwavering.

Response to "Gunning for It" from
LIEUTENANT BRIAN THIEM,
Oakland Police Department, Retired

Rebecca Morgan Frank's poem stirred my emotions. Good poetry does that.

I spent thirty years in law enforcement and saw gun violence firsthand: Hundreds of murder victims lying dead in streets, cars, homes, and city parks. Many hundreds more who were wounded and survived—at least physically.

The problem with the emphasis on the gun part of gun violence is it ignores the human component. Targeting guns is easier than targeting those who use them unlawfully and those who protect the shooters.

Mao Tse-Tung said, "The guerrilla must move amongst the people as a fish swims in the sea." In our inner cities, where gun violence is epidemic, shooters move among the citizens with impunity. Neighborhood residents know who they are, but they look the other way. During political protests, black-masked anarchists shoot guns and throw firebombs, then meld back into the crowd, while the "peaceful" protesters look the other way.

More signs on doors reading *No Firearms Permitted* and laws limiting guns to ten-round magazines won't solve the problem. Criminals already disobey laws prohibiting murder.

Don't get me wrong—I support gun control, but until our society stops excusing violence and ignoring those committing the acts, the problem will not subside.

The Bullet, in Its Hunger

ROSS GAY

The bullet, in its hunger, craves the womb
of the body. The warm thrum there. Begs always
release from the chilly, dumb chamber.
Look at this one whose glee
at escape was outshone only by the heavens
above him. The night's even-keeled
breath. All things thus far dreams from
his cramped bunker. But now
the world. Let me be a ravenous diamond
in it, he thinks, chewing through the milky jawbone
of this handsome seventeen-year-old. Of course
he would love to nestle amidst the brain's
scintillant catacombs (which, only for the boy's dumb luck,
slipped away) but this will do. The bullet does
not, as the boy goes into shock, or as his best friend
stutters, palming the fluid wound, want to know the nature
of the conflict, nor the sound of the shooter's
mother in prayer, nor the shot child's future harmonies:
the tracheotomy's muffled wheeze
threaded through the pencil's whisper as the boy scrawls I'm
scared. No,
the bullet, like you, simply craves
the warmth of the body. Like you, only wants
to die in someone's arms.

Response to "The Bullet, in Its Hunger"
from WILLIAM V. BEGG III, MD FACEP,
Treating Emergency Room Doctor for
Sandy Hook Elementary School Tragedy

The bullet will be in charge no longer.

Prior to the Sandy Hook tragedy, most medical professionals like me stood by and let bullets ravage American citizens. When the bullet is in charge, it only has one goal, which is to destroy the human body as well as the spirit of mankind. After the Sandy Hook tragedy, we Americans led by common sense and our medical professionals are now in charge. Gun violence is a public health issue, and we will tolerate no longer shedding tears needlessly. Just like the changes we made addressing the cigarettes and drunk drivers that took so many lives in the last generation, the next generation of young Americans has the burden of making those changes necessary to make gun deaths a thing of the past. Witnessing the unnecessary loss of life of so many young children and educators who were my neighbors and friends makes one inspired to never give up fighting to decrease the number of gun violence deaths in our country. We are on the right side of history.

The bullet is in charge no longer.

[11 Gunshots]

VANESSA GERMAN

11 gunshots woke me up dis morning.6:32am.i count them.
bangbangbangbangbangand on and on right there. right out
in front of the house or. sound throws itself around it cdda
been the alleyway.but.anyways.it was right here.right there.
the way that it feels to me iz first a feeling to the stomach.my
hand went to my stomach and i crouched down.had been in
the prep stages of leaving the house to head to the gym.only
then. alla those gun shots. and i count them.it iz an impossible
thing to not.count the gun shots. and thank god. no screams.
and no tire screeching.i think that screams wd have rendered
me. a new creature. but no screams. and no more shots after
the first 11. i crawled over to the window to check the street.
for a body. for a silent fall. for a face down man. with hiz tennis
shoes still on. that's the rub. that. when it's so close. you have
to check for a body. peeking from corner of window. i see.
no. body. so i go on wit myself. i. sit down. i can't find the cell
phone. i hear nothing. else on the street. i check the street
again. because alla those shots. were so mean and so close. the
street iz long and quiet and black at this hour in the morning.
perhaps there were bus waiters? but not dis morning. what else
cd i tell you. i waz afraid to leave the house after that. i haven't
been afraid to leave the house since mr. ___ waz murdered.
8 shots and alla those screams. so many screams that the 911
operator had to raise hiz voice. tell me. in the calm calming
sound. ma'am. ma'am. you're gonna have to stop screaming.
and i tell him. no sir. i am not screaming. the woman on the

street. iz. and so. this morning i waz afraid to go out to the car. to sit in it on the street. to do the waiting of ignition to warm up. i didn't want to be found. just sitting there. waiting. when it seems like lately there haz been a war going on. 5 shootings on wednesday. homicide detectives waving to me in their men's warehouse rack suits. waving to me. and racing. the middle school kids cut through the field the other day. hacking at the concrete wit their rush n panic. _____ lookin over her shoulder every 5 steps. their faces. like. brave. fleers. az though someone told them. this is what brave looks like. and they wear that face. i ask her. i say. what's going on. she says. they're shooting. they're shooting over there. i say, the kids she says. no. a man. looking. looking over her shoulder 4 or 5 times in that brief exchange. the group cuts through another alleyway. the helicopters r circling. ghetto birds. police hawks. avian predators. they'd been up in the sky for 20 minutes by this time. the street waz a live with gun shots. a man i'd never seen before. face tattoos ill-fitting denim and that same way the kids were looking over their shoulders he waz too. an over the shoulder stalker wit. sights. in hiz eyes. i say what's going on he iz walking like he iz walking. Away. from a thing that needed. to be walked Away from. he says. shooting. i say. shooting. he says. a man. i say. is he ok. the man looks at me funny and says. he's dead. then a rental car pulls up in the middle of the street. and this man gets into it. the rental car brought to mind the kitten-heeled homicide detective who. under her breath declared. of mr. ____'s killer. we'll never find him. she said. they were in a rental car. they'll dump it. we will never find them. and the afternoon school buses came late. lock down. and some of the kids. haven't been the same since. well. you know. only. maybe you don't. perhaps there iz the grand assumption that we're all on the same page with this heat and blood and street and screaming and waking up to the fire of a gun. and. no one knows the language of these mornings the way that we do. how do you walk the child to the bus stop. who will call the fourth grade teacher. to tell them. listen. today. _____ is going to be different. may need. more. ____. or. ___. please. accommodate this trauma. with. more. love and deep listening. i am not strong enuf. to keep rising to mornings with the gunshots. my heart. iz az soft after the dawn following storm promises. i am not strong enuf. to just take it. swallow it down. my body does not like the sound of gun shots. my soul reels with concern for all of us. one of. the grandmothers tells me of her. despair. the deep depression she tells in quiet voice at bus stop bench red. in front of the arthouse she says. that she can not even stand. to lookit. the walls sometimes. every room must be dark she says. she haz been to the land of unbearable. and has barely made it back. i am thinking about strength. i am thinking about strength and i do not know what it is. i don't know its face. i am thinking about. love. and i know what love's face looks like. i am thinking about how and why.it could be so safe. 6 blocks away under the railroad tracks. and. that is ok. it iz ok to be there. to place your child into the bed. safe. there. but not here. and how. maybe they'd put the dogs on me. maybe. they'd say. that this is more of what iz deserved. you people. you people you people. i am thinking about strength. and the sun shine. and how despair looks when it iz holding a 9. i am thinking about the weekend sunshine. and how some people will relish the sunshine. golden. at a city park. and others will.

i will move about with hope. a sure marrow in my limbs. that. no one wants to gun it out this weekend. just because the sun is shining. i don't know what else to tell you that isn't primarily. about. love. i fought very hard. to love myself with grace and discipline today. i worked out. i have eaten fruit. i drank the water. i sent love notes to my friends. and it's only 2pm. and. mostly. it's love. now. i put those 11 gunshots into the temporary storage of. grief. sorrow.trauma.deep pain. and healing. that love haz carved out between my fingers and my rib bones. i am lucky to be an artist. _____ has blessed me. with a wild imagination. and studio space. i know. that these won't be the last.shots that we hear. i know. i know. what i am saying now. iz. that i have found a love space. that iz wiser than language. my mother's song iz in there. az iz the sound of my ancestors being ancestors. so. i'm going to work now. i love. i art. i healing.

February 5, 2016

◀ *Response to "[11 Gunshots]" from*
CAMIELLA WILLIAMS, *Gun Reform Activist*

Are we talking the sexy gun violence or the ugly gun violence? I ask as a woman under thirty years old who has witnessed nearly thirty loved ones killed but has no form of treatment to help her cope with her trauma, who lives with PTSD like a person in a war! Are we talking sexy gun violence when a nation stops to ring bells and elected officials give speeches and call for gun sense, or are we talking the ugly gun violence where three children under thirteen are shot dead on the streets of Chicago, Cleveland, and Detroit, and all we get is that's so SAD our thoughts and prayers are with the family meanwhile let's march to protect everything but our black and brown babies? Are we talking the ugly gun violence where people can't commute back and forth or even be outside without fear of being killed? Are we talking sexy gun violence where a school is demolished to remove the painful memories or are we talking the ugly gun violence where children have to play on a blood-stained playground, or where people go to class to hear their classmate was killed over the weekend while they have a test? Are we talking the sexy gun violence where counselors stay around the clock for weeks? People say gun violence is gun violence, but where I am from it's the ugly gun violence where it seems no one gives a damn! It's hell—in order not to be scared you have to not be afraid to die.

Dancing

ROBERT HASS

The radio clicks on—it's poor swollen America,
Up already and busy selling the exhausting obligation
Of happiness while intermittently debating whether or not
A man who kills fifty people in five minutes
With an automatic weapon he has bought for the purpose
Is mentally ill. Or a terrorist. Or if terrorists
Are mentally ill. Because if killing large numbers of people
With sophisticated weapons is a sign of sickness—
You might want to begin with fire, our early ancestors
Drawn to the warmth of it—from lightning,
Must have been, the great booming flashes of it
From the sky, the tree shriveled and sizzling,
Must have been, an awful power, the odor
Of ozone a god's breath; or grass fires,
The wind whipping them, the animals stampeding,
Furious, driving hard on their haunches from the terror
Of it, so that to fashion some campfire of burning wood,
Old logs, must have felt like feeding on the crumbs
Of the god's power and they would tell the story
Of Prometheus the thief, and the eagle that feasted
On his liver, told it around a campfire, must have been,
And then—centuries, millennia—some tribe
Of meticulous gatherers, some medicine woman,
Or craftsman of metal discovered some sands that,
Tossed into the fire, burned blue or flared green,
So simple the children could do it, must have been,

Or some soft stone rubbed to a powder that tossed
Into the fire gave off a white phosphorescent glow.
The word for *chemistry* from a Greek—some say Arabic—
Stem associated with metal work. But it was in China
Two thousand years ago that fireworks were invented—
Fire and mineral in a confined space to produce power—
They knew already about the power of fire and water
And the power of steam: 100 BC, Julius Caesar's day.
In Alexandria, a Greek mathematician produced
A steam-powered turbine engine. Contain, explode.
"The earliest depiction of a gunpowder weapon
Is the illustration of a fire-lance on a mid-12th-century
Silk banner from Dunhuang." Silk and the silk road.
First Arab guns in the early fourteenth century. The English
Used cannons and a siege gun at Calais in 1346.
Cerigna, 1503: the first battle won by the power of rifles
When Spanish "arquebusiers" cut down Swiss pikemen
And French cavalry in a battle in southern Italy.
(Explosions of blood and smoke, lead balls tearing open
The flesh of horses and young men, peasants mostly,
Farm boys recruited to the armies of their feudal overlords.)
How did guns come to North America? 2014,
A headline: DIVERS DISCOVER THE SANTA MARIA.
One of the ship's Lombard cannons may have been stolen
By salvage pirates off the Haitian reef where it had sunk.
And Cortes took Mexico with 600 men, 17 horses, 12 cannons.
And LaSalle, 1679, constructed a seven-cannon barque,
Le Griffon, and fired his cannons upon first entering the
    continent's
Interior. The sky darkened by the terror of the birds.

In the dream time, they are still rising, swarming,
Darkening the sky, the chorus of their cries sharpening
As the echo of that first astounding explosion shimmers
On the waters, the crew blinking at the wind of their wings.
Springfield Arsenal, 1777. Rock Island Arsenal, 1862.
The original Henry rifle: a sixteen shot .44 caliber rimfire
Lever-action, breech-loading rifle patented—it was an age
Of tinkerers—by one Benjamin Tyler Henry in 1860,
Just in time for the Civil War. Confederate casualties
In battle: about 95,000. Union casualties in battle:
About 110,000. Contain, explode. They were throwing
Sand into the fire, a blue flare, an incandescent green.
The Maxim machine gun, 1914, 400-600 small caliber rounds
Per minute. The deaths in combat, all sides, 1914-1918
Was 8,042,189. Someone was counting. Must have been.
They could send things whistling into the air by boiling water.
The children around the fire must have shrieked with delight.
1920: Iraq, the peoples of that place were "restive,"
Under British rule and the young Winston Churchill
Invented the new policy of "aerial policing," which amounted,
Sources say, to bombing civilians and then pacifying them
With ground troops. Which led to the tactic of terrorizing
    civilian
Populations in World War II. Total casualties in that war,
Worldwide: soldiers, 21 million; civilians, 27 million.
They were throwing sand into the fire. The ancestor who stole
Lightning from the sky had his guts eaten by an eagle.
Spread-eagled on a rock, the great bird feasting.
They are wondering if he is a terrorist or mentally ill.
London, Dresden. Berlin. Hiroshima, Nagasaki.

The casualties difficult to estimate. Hiroshima:
66,000 dead, 70,000 injured. In a minute. Nagasaki:
39,000 dead, 25,000 injured . There were more people killed,
100,000, in more terrifying fashion in the firebombing
Of Tokyo. Two arms races after the ashes settled.
The other industrial countries couldn't get there
Fast enough. Contain, burn. One scramble was
For the rocket that delivers the explosion that burns humans
By the tens of thousands and poisons the earth in the process.
They were wondering if the terrorist was crazy. If he was
A terrorist, maybe he was just unhappy. The other
Challenge afterwards was how to construct machine guns
A man or a boy could carry: lightweight, compact, easy to
    assemble.
First a Russian sergeant, a Kalashnikov, clever with guns
Built one on a German model. Now the heavy machine gun,
The weapon of European imperialism through which
A few men trained in gunnery could slaughter native armies
In Africa and India and the mountains of Afghanistan,
Became "a portable weapon a child can operate."
The equalizer. So the undergunned Vietnamese insurgents
Fought off the greatest army in the world. So the Afghans
Fought off the Soviet army using Kalashnikovs the CIA
Provided to them. They were throwing powders in the fire
And dancing. Children's armies in Africa toting AK-47s
That fire thirty rounds a minute. A round is a bullet.
An estimated 500 million firearms on the earth.
100 million of them are Kalashnikov-style semi-automatics.
They were dancing in Orlando, in a club. Spring night.
Gay Pride. The relation of the total casualties to the history

Of the weapon that sent exploded metal into their bodies—
30 rounds a minute, or 40, is a beautifully made instrument,
And in America you can buy it anywhere—and into the history
Of the shaming culture that produced the idea of Gay Pride—
They were mostly young men, they were dancing in a club,
A spring night. The radio clicks on. Green fire. Blue fire.
The immense flocks of terrified birds still rising
In wave after wave above the waters in the dream time.
Crying out sharply. As the French ship breasted the vast
    interior
Of the new land. America. A radio clicks on. The Arabs,
A commentator is saying, require a heavy hand. Dancing.

Response to "Dancing" from Jody Williams, *Nobel Peace Prize Laureate and Cofounder of the Nobel Women's Initiative*

I've worked in and around war and weapons since 1981—guns, landmines, cluster bombs, nuclear bombs, and, now, killer robots. Killer robots, on the verge of engaging in battle on their own without human intervention, are being called the third "revolution" in warfare: gun powder, nukes, and now killer machines that on their own can target and kill human beings.

Upon learning about killer robots a group of us who had worked to ban landmines and cluster bombs formed a new campaign to stop killer robots. At its root is a fundamental repugnance at the thought that some people actually believe it is morally and ethically perfectly fine to create machines to find, target, and kill other people. So much for the often-heard pro-gun argument that guns don't kill people, people kill people.

I love the myth of Prometheus stealing fire—stealing some of the god Zeus's power—for the benefit of humans. I'd like to rewrite it for our times. In my version, Prometheus would steal gunpowder, nuclear weapons, and the makings of killer robots and bury them deep in a cave on Mt. Olympus. To save human beings from ourselves.

Poem by Poem

JUAN FELIPE HERRERA

—in memory of
Cynthia Hurd, Susie Jackson, Ethel Lance,
Rev. Depayne Middleton-Doctor,
Hon. Rev. Clementa Pinckney,
Tywanza Sanders, Rev. Daniel Simmons Sr.,
Rev. Sharonda Singleton, Myra Thompson
Shot and killed while at church.
Charleston, SC (6-18-2015), RIP

        poem by   poem
we can end the violence
every day   after
    every other day
9 killed in Charleston, South Carolina
they are not 9 they
are each one
        alive
we do not know
    you have a poem to offer
it is made of action—you must
search for it   run
outside and give your life to it
when you find it   walk it
back—blow upon it
carry it taller than the city where you live

when the blood comes down
do not ask   if
          it is your blood   it
is made of
          9   drops
                    honor them
wash them stop them
from falling

Response to "Poem by Poem" from
THE REVEREND SHARON RISHER, *Survivor*
of Multiple Victims in the Emanuel African
Methodist Episcopal Church Shootings in
Charleston, South Carolina, on June 17, 2015

My heart raced as I tried to clear my head and heart to read this poem about the senseless deaths of my mother, two cousins, and a childhood friend. Just like now. I'm shaking like I have never read it. I've read it ten times or more and, still, it's like the first time.

The day it happened was just like any other day. The Bible study went on as usual. Then evil lurked and entered this sacred place. These souls died together, yet they have their own stories. Please don't forget that—individuals each one.

Momma, Ethel Lance, loved fine perfumes and liked things to be decent and in order at all times—her home and her job. She took pride in caring for them both.

Mrs. Susie Jackson—infectious smile, love for all her family members. Matriarch of the church. Always watching to make sure you were behaving in "God's house."

Tywanza Sanders—full of life, trying to make space in the world through his artistic and entrepreneurial gifts.

Myra Singleton, my childhood friend. During the summer breaks, we would play school and Myra was always a teacher. She spent her life as a teacher. It was already in her way back then.

Throwing a Life Line

BOB HICOK

Say you're a professor and one of your students
shot and killed thirty-two people.
Say it's years later. Fall's begun and kids
have that eager look of tulips in their faces,
of green life pushing up from the ground
toward sun. In the smile of one passing,
you see the joy of one who passed,
one of the thirty-two, and follow her
with your imagination. You give her life
in a poem by having her run along a beach,
her children behind her and their grandparents
behind them, everyone wanting dinner,
everyone wanting stars to come out
and be their silly, shiny selves, everyone wanting
that next little breath. But let me ask—
are you drinking again? Have you driven your car
into a tree? Do you have a suicide note
for a heart? Do you wake on the wrong side
of the bed—the bottom, not the top?
Say you're so desperate for gun control
that you're thinking of appealing to conservatives
by suggesting that murder is abortion
when one considers the children this woman
was likely to have had, the children
you just gave her in your poem
but are in danger of killing

if you let your anger take that political turn.
Don't do it. Don't you see that poems
make horrible legislation and even worse
bullet-proof vests, so brittle
and thin-skinned? Just let her live.
Let her run with the kite of her children
behind her. That's what I'd do
if I were you. And the drinking.
The driving into trees. I'd do those too.
I'd drink and crash and write one poem
for every day of her life. Hell. I'd drink more
and crash better and write two.

Response to "Throwing a Life Line" from
COLIN GODDARD, *Survivor of the 2007*
Virginia Tech Shootings and Gun Violence
Prevention Advocate

We must challenge any politician who thinks it's easier to ask an elementary school teacher to stand up to a gunman with an AR-15 than it is to ask themselves to stand up to a gun lobbyist with a checkbook.

The Family Sells the Family Gun

BRENDA HILLMAN

a prose ballad

i only held it once but thought about it often as you think
    about those times when your life had stood both loaded &
    unloaded

One brother knew of its existence having seen it where it
    languished in the famed green storage unit from which it
    had been transferred to the bank-box but we never quite
    knew when

Information our father had & something he was squeamish
    about or proud of at the same time the way Protestants are
    about genitals

We believed it was a Luger—maybe taken from a soldier—
    in the War our father trained for but didn't ever get to
    because he was wounded in the knee—"sustained" is
    the word they use—sustained a wound—in infantry
    maneuvers before his men were mostly killed after
    D-Day—

When his ashes in the desert grave were lying we took the
    weapon from the bank-box

i put it quickly in my handbag to get it past the teller—the
   holster was the smoothest leather—brown & heavy—the
   yawning L-shape of the Luger Google says Georg Luger
   designed in 1898—the holster smooth as the jackets of
   German soldiers in the movies & what had they done to
   make the cowhide smooth like that & what had they done
   to the cow

We thought of burying it in the desert but if you Google
   burying a firearm it changes to a search for *buying a firearm*

You can also look up how to load a semi-automatic weapon
   on YouTube where a white man with thick hands & a
   wedding band shows you how to check for rounds in what
   order & tells you how to handle it with your dominant
   hand

We couldn't take it to the cops even in my handbag though
   Arizona is open carry & you can take it anywhere in
   public but the cops can shoot you if you take your gun to
   their station

One young Tucson cop named Matt agreed to come to us
   & checked the magazine & said it was unloaded—looked
   upon us with excruciatingly mild pity—said this relic
   might be worth some money & stroked it the way some
   boys do

i couldn't tell what the brothers were thinking—it felt like a
   tragedy but reversible—our father's ghost stood like a tall
   working summer like Hamlet's father's ghost appearing
   only in the day & good naturedly telling people not do the
   killing but still trying to control the actions of the play

You can think about ghostly word weapons non-stop   Let's
   just take a shot at it   She was going great guns   He loved
   her but couldn't quite pull the trigger Better to just bite
   the bullet   Kill an hour or two

& for some reason maybe sorrow for our father's power/lack
   of power i felt a twinge when my brother whisked the
   tiny heavy out of there—my life had stood a secret little
   hiddenly shameful semi-automatic firearm & *When at*
   night Our good day done i guard my Master's head

My younger brother sold it for $600 to a Tucson gun shop—
   one of those outfits where the master paces behind the
   counter offering advice on collecting & is so proud of his
   stash

It was a Tuesday i think—a Tuesday inside history where
   America is lost—& what should we do with the cash

Response to "The Family Sells the Family Gun"
from JENNIFER MASCIA, *Author of* Never Tell
Our Business to Strangers

My father killed people. Not with knives or explosives or bows and arrows but with guns. Guns made it easy for him to take life. Without the invention of guns, my father's drug-dealing career might never have had a body count. (Without the invention of guns, I probably wouldn't be writing this.) What might he have been in this alternate reality? In a world without guns, would he have been an electrician (his dream career, until some idiot teacher told him to dream another dream because he wasn't the best at math)? Would he have been a lawyer (he'd been a jailhouse lawyer during his time at Sing Sing and was adept at composing legal briefs)? In a world without guns, perhaps he wouldn't have been defined by the worst thing he ever did. Because even though he's my father—and he was a good father to me, and even though cancer took him fifteen years ago, I still love him—now that I know his secrets, it's hard to ever un-know them. And perhaps, in a world without guns, he wouldn't have been Dad, the Killer. In a world without guns, maybe he'd just have been Dad.

Those Who Cannot Act

JANE HIRSHFIELD

"Those who act will suffer,
suffer into truth"—
What Aeschylus omitted:
those who cannot act will suffer too.

The sister banished into exile.
The unnamed dog
soon killed.

Even the bystanders vanish,
one by one,
peripheral, in pain unnoticed while

Response to "Those Who Cannot Act" from
US Senator Chris Murphy, Connecticut

How can Congress continue to sleep at night when, five years after the murder of twenty first-graders and six educators in their school, nothing has been done to stop the cascading waves of gun violence across America? We cannot accept the daily carnage in our streets. Getting shot while worshiping in church or watching a movie with loved ones cannot be the new normal.

Silence from Congress in the wake of gun violence has become complicity. We don't even try to make our communities safer—and that's what's most offensive. Last year, over thirty thousand of our brothers, sisters, fathers, and mothers were gunned down. And Congress has done absolutely nothing. Instead, we keep sending a loud signal that we just don't care about this epidemic of preventable murder in our country.

The only way we change this reality is if people speak up, consistently and loudly. Ask yourself: what can you do to make sure that Orlando, or Aurora, or Sandy Hook never happens again? It can't be solely thoughts and prayers buried in tweets or in moments of silence. We must continue to speak out—to tell the stories of loved ones lost and to push for action to save lives.

Gatorland

LEANNE HOWE

I have Herpetophobia.

!   Fear of alligators roaming the streets once Trump
       drains the swamp

? How to recognize these wild beasts

!   There's her, that foul-mouthed sexter, a hard-
       drinking blonde who learned to breathe heavily just
       so people in the next room could hear. A friend.

       And Him, horsetail hair, orange body paint.
       His family, settlers in eveningwear, they constitute
       a high-heeled army in service to the super-rich.
       Straight shooters.

!   See her #2,
       The sleek suited hedge-fund type, she tells me
       She carries a Glock 9 mm. Fears everything
       Complains her swan furniture flirts with strangers,
       It's the meds.

       There goes another creature in a black cocktail dress
       Without a handgun
       Well-heeled propriety
       Won't last long

!   Not as chichi as the
       Bald woman wearing chandelier earrings striking a pose
       in the white fur coat
       She says she shot the foxes herself. She fears hair.
       Shoots at it in the dark.
       Needs meds.

): I have Herpetophobia

?!   Don't be a moron, who ever heard of an American
       Indian Herpetophobic

Maybe I'll sign up for an alligator wrestling class
Carry a gun
Turn killer with a song in my heart
      As did the drunks and vagrants posing as settlers,
Nattering across our homelands like a proverb, singing "Holy,
    Holy, Holy"
Or maybe I'll forget who I am, party with alligators,
      Dine on the dead, breath reeking of poison

?   You're making me horny, can you tell me more

⊙ *Settlers carried a little bit of heaven into battle, the Hawken rifle*
    Sang "Just As I Am" with a Colt 45 in their hands
    Killing Indians face-to-face was a blast

:)   Don't stop, I'm getting off, *oh . . . oh*

For long-range slaughter they dragged Big Fifty onto the field
A big girl rifle weighing 17 pounds, she fired .50/120 rounds
⊙
  ⊙
   ⊙
⊙
Big Fifty was used at the battle of Adobe Walls. Felled Indians
   1500 yards away

Settlers, cavalrymen, sheriffs, deputies, peacekeepers used
Spencers, the .56-50 caliber
Henry Repeating Arms
Winchester '66
Winchester '73s

!   Thanks, I needed that

): *Maybe we're all Indians these days*

:)   Now you're talking

I have Herpetophobia

!   Nonsense, buy a gun and kill it

Response to "Gatorland" from AMANDA GAILEY,
Nebraskans Against Gun Violence

The National Rifle Association was the largest investor in
the Trump campaign. Trump is the pure distillation of the
NRA's ethos: that true Americanness is white, male, Chris-
tian, and armed. We need guns to fight tyranny they say,
standing on land won by armed genocide, farmed by slavery
enforced by arms, next to women they view as sexual prop-
erty and guard with guns, staring down the barrel of a gun at
refugees and immigrants.

But tyranny is the gun. Guns are the monetizable form
of the white male Christianist myth of America. Guns are
the lie that violence begets peace: imperialist violence, manly
violence, religious violence. Guns are the lie that the daily
count of the dead matters less than the fantasies of dupes
who give their paychecks and children to gun manufacturers.
Guns are the tools of the otherwise untooled, and when the
only tool you have is a gun, every answer to every problem
is to shoot it.

Ferguson

MAJOR JACKSON

Once there was a boy who thought it a noble idea to lie down in the middle of the street and sleep. For four hours, no one bothered him, but let him lie on the road as though he were an enchantment. This became newsworthy and soon helicopters hovered above, hosing his curled torso and thick legs in spotlights televised the world over. Foreign correspondents focused on the neighborhood and its relative poverty as recognized by the plethora of low-hanging jeans worn by shirtless men and loud music issuing from passing cars, which had the effect of drowning out everyone's already bottled-up thoughts about the boy sleeping in the middle of the street; others jumped in front of cameras seizing an opportunity to be seen by their relatives on the other side of town because they had run out of minutes on prepaid cellphones.

The roadkill in the neighborhood, and some on that very block, rodents, cats, and possums, feeling equal amounts of jealousy and futility, each began to rise and return to their den holes, cursing the boy sleeping in the street beneath their breaths for his virtuosic performance of stillness and tribulation in the city. The drug-addicted men and women leaning into doorways like art installations were used to being ignored, but they, too, felt affronted by the boy sleeping in the street and folded their cardboard homes.

For the first hour, he practiced not breathing. For ten seconds, he would hold his breath. And then, he practiced longer sets of minutes during the next three hours until he was able to stretch out his non-breathing for whole hunks at a time. When his breathing returned, it was so faint, his chest and shoulders barely moved; infinitesimal amounts of life poured out of him, but no one noticed. The police cordoned off his body, and after some time, declared him dead because they had only seen black men lying prone on the street as corpses, but never as sleeping humans.

The whole world, eager and hungry for a Lazarus moment, watched and waited to see when he would awaken and rise to his feet, especially his neighbors with minutes remaining on cellphones who filmed and animatedly discoursed behind yellow tape the ecstasies and muted sorrows of watching a boy sleep in the middle of the street.

◀ *Response to "Ferguson" from* AMBER GOODWIN,
Founder and Executive Director of
Community Justice Reform Coalition

Ferguson changed everything. This poem exemplifies that fact but was equal parts hard to read and to digest—just like Ferguson. I think this poem tried to look at Michael Brown, who for once was referred to as an actual human, not just a victim or body. Or at least tried to get there. I think this was a way to try to humanize such an inhuman action that happened that day due to gun violence. On the other hand: How do we deal with the inhumane action of the words in this writing and what actually happened? Or is the actual question Do we ever deal with it? Lord only knows, but we have to talk about it in ways that will never forgive what happened and also will never forget the uprising and spark that followed. It changed me. It changed this country. Ferguson changed everything.

The Talking Day

MICHAEL KLEIN

Some lunatic with a gun killed some people at an immigration center in Binghamton, New York. Liz Rosenberg and her family live up there and David, her husband, teaches in the middle school which is close to all the action (the way, in any smallish town, everything is close to all the action). I called Liz to see if everyone was all right and she was in her car driving to the elementary school to pick up Lily, her young daughter she brought back from China a few years ago. Lily was fine, but Liz wanted to move her outside the question of how to make sense of the broken pieces of "someone" with a gun walking into a public space and then firing. There's something called (I learned from a news report the day of the shootings at Virginia Tech) The Talking Day which refers to the day immediately following the day when something wildly violent happens. No one quite grasps the reality of the situation and everyone spends that first day talking about what happened and reliving it as language— not so much to understand the violence but to make a kind of recording of it: talking about it, letting go of it, putting it down. And so I imagine it must be with Liz and Lily and David in Binghamton, New York today: letting "something" go. Liz is in her car after having just picked up

Lily at school and driving back home through a town that suddenly makes no sense and she is telling the story about what happened when a young man walked into a building with a gun. And for Lily, who's had a pretty serene, un-violent United States time so far and whose endless joy has made her an adorable chatterbox, tomorrow could be her first talking day. Or, if not tomorrow, some other day. We live in a talking day world.

Response to "The Talking Day" from
MONTE FRANK, *Founder of Team 26*
(www.team26.org)

I live in Sandy Hook with my family and a dog. Every morning, I wake up at the crack of dawn, brew a pot of coffee, and look out through my wooded backyard as the sun rises. This is the quiet quintessential New England town I sought out to raise my girls and to live peacefully. It was the town no one had heard of until it was plastered all over the news, all over the world. Twenty-six murdered. Twenty children executed in their first-grade classrooms. We call that day 12/14. It is our 9/11. It's the day our world changed forever. More than four years later, I'm still searching for that Talking Day, a day when I can put it down and let it go. Given what happened here, I'm not sure that day will ever come.

Shotguns

YUSEF KOMUNYAKAA

The day after Christmas
Blackbirds lifted like a shadow
Of an oak, slow leaves
Returning to bare branches.
We followed them, a hundred
Small premeditated murders
Clustered in us like happiness.
We had the scent of girls
On our hands & in our mouths,
Moving like jackrabbits from one
Dream to the next. Brand-new
Barrels shone against the day
& stole wintery light
From trees. In the time it took
To run home & grab Daddy's gun,
The other wing-footed boys
Stumbled from the woods.
Johnny Lee was all I heard,
A siren in the flesh,
The name of a fallen friend
In their wild throats. Only Joe
Stayed to lift Johnny's head
Out of the ditch, rocking back
& forth. The first thing I did
Was to toss the shotgun

Into a winterberry thicket,
& didn't know I was running
To guide the paramedics into
The dirt-green hush. We sat
In a wordless huddle outside
The operating room, till a red light
Over the door began pulsing
Like a broken vein in a skull.

Response to "Shotguns" from DeAndra Yates,
*Mother of Dre, Advocate, and Founder of
Purpose 4 My Pain*

One Shot One Bullet changed my life forever. To hear that your innocent, your love, your baby . . . had taken a bullet to the head is indescribable. A pain that no mother should feel, but one that mothers are feeling now on a daily basis. My oldest of two children, Dre, was only thirteen when a stray bullet pierced the back of his head while attending a birthday party. The bullet flew in through a window, from outside gunfire. . . . The shooter has yet to be apprehended. . . . Circumstances are still unclear.

The pain of Dre's shooting shook me and my family to the core. But in the midst of my pain, my heart desired to find purpose. When I heard the words "you should let him go" or "it's not about you, it's about the quality of life that he would want to live," a fight rose up in me. I prayed and said God create a path for me to find purpose. On this journey, I've decided to become a voice for those who have been silenced too soon. Particularly those that have been injured. To let my nonverbal child stand as a beacon of hope for the hopeless . . . to fight so that Dre's life-altering tragedy will not be in vain and so that our shooter will never feel as if he took the best of us . . . he only helped manifest it.

Instructions for Stopping

DANA LEVIN

Say *Stop*.

Keep your lips pressed together
after you say the *p*:

(soon they'll try
and pry

your breath out—)

—

Whisper it
three times in a row:

Stop Stop Stop—

In a hospital bed
like a curled-up fish, someone's

gulping at air—

How should you apply
your breath?

—

List all of the people
you would like
to stop.

Who offers love,
who terror—

Write *Stop*.
Put a period at the end.

Decide if it's a kiss
or a bullet.

Response to "Instructions for Stopping" from
KATE RANTA, *Domestic and Gun Violence Survivor,*
Cofounder of Women Against the Violence Epidemic

I was on the floor like a curled-up fish, yelling *Stop Stop Stop*. November 2, 2012, the date that changed my life and my family's lives forever. My ex-husband appeared at my apartment door and shot my father and me. In front of my then-four-year-old son. The son I had with my ex-husband. His own son. My right hand exploded in front of my eyes. *STOP!* A bullet went through my left chest. *STOP!* A bullet was shot point blank into my father's left side. *STOP!* I slid in my own blood and begged for my life. "Don't do it, Daddy! Don't shoot Mommy!" That's what my son said, as I lay curled up. Make no mistake: Bullets hurt. Bullets kill. Domestic abusers with guns shoot bullets that hurt. That kill. I survived. My father survived. My son survived. The physical wounds healed. But the psychological scars are lifelong. *Stop* abusers. Now.

The Leash

ADA LIMÓN

After the birthing of bombs of forks and fear,
the frantic automatic weapons unleashed,
the spray of bullets into a crowd holding hands,
that brute sky opening in a slate metal maw
that swallows only the unsayable in each of us, what's
left? Even the hidden nowhere river is poisoned
orange and acidic by a coal mine. How can
you not fear humanity, want to lick the creek
bottom dry to suck the deadly water up into
your own lungs, like venom? Reader, I want to
say, *Don't die.* Even when silvery fish after fish
comes back belly up, and the country plummets
into a crepitating crater of hatred, isn't there still
something singing? The truth is: I don't know.
But sometimes, I swear I hear it, the wound closing
like a rusted-over garage door, and I can still move
my living limbs into the world without too much
pain, can still marvel at how the dog runs straight
toward the pickup trucks break-necking down
the road, because she thinks she loves them,
because she's sure, without a doubt, that the loud
roaring things will love her back, her soft small self
alive with desire to share her goddamn enthusiasm,
until I yank the leash back to save her because
I want her to survive forever. *Don't die,* I say,
and we decide to walk for a bit longer, starlings

high and fevered above us, winter coming to lay
her cold corpse down upon this little plot of earth.
Perhaps we are always hurtling our body towards
the thing that will obliterate us, begging for love
from the speeding passage of time, and so maybe
like the dog obedient at my heels, we can walk together
peacefully, at least until the next truck comes.

Response to "The Leash" from CAREN TEVES,
Mother of Alex Teves, Killed in the Aurora,
Colorado, Shooting

July 20, 2012, 12:38 a.m.: A twenty-four-year-old white male enters an Aurora Cinemark movie theater through an un-alarmed security door. Fueled by a self-admitted desire for infamy and armed with three guns and six thousand rounds of ammunition that he easily and legally obtained, despite his past and current mental health history, he begins shooting with the intent to kill everyone.

In the rear of the theater, another twenty-four-year-old man performs a selfless act of love. Knowing the risk to himself, he immediately pulls his girlfriend to the floor using his body to successfully shield her when he is hit in the forehead with a single armor-piercing bullet, violently ending his life.

My husband, Tom, and I were not surprised by the heroic actions of our first-born son, Alex Teves. He was always kind and fiercely protected those he loved. We miss him every moment of every day. Alex is one of over thirty thousand people killed annually with guns in the United States.

The quest for fame is a well-known motivating factor in rampage mass killings. Upon learning this, we founded NoNotoriety.com, calling for responsible media coverage of these killers in an effort to save lives.

Kablooey is the Sound You'll Hear

DEBRA MARQUART

then plaster falling and the billow of gypsum
after your sister blows a hole in the ceiling
of your brother's bedroom with the shotgun
he left loaded and resting on his dresser.

It's Saturday, and the men are in the fields.
You and your sister are cleaning house
with your mother. Maybe your sister hates
cleaning that much, or maybe she's just

that thorough, but somehow she has lifted
the gun to dust it or dust under it (you are busy
mopping the stairs) and from the top landing
where you stand, you turn toward the sound

to see your sister cradling the smoking shotgun
in her surprised arms, like a beauty queen
clutching a bouquet of long-stemmed roses
after being pronounced the official winner.

Then the smell of burnt gunpowder
reaches you, dirty orange and sulfurous,
like spent fireworks, and through the veil
of smoke you see a hole smoldering

above her head, a halo of perforations
in the ceiling—the drywall blown clean

through insulation to naked joists, that dark
constellation where the buckshot spread.

The look on your sister's face is pure
shitfaced shock. You'd like to stop and
photograph it for blackmail or future
family stories but now you must focus

on the face of your mother, frozen at the base
of the stairs where she has rushed from
vacuuming or waxing, her frantic eyes
searching your face for some clue

about the extent of the catastrophe.
But it's like that heavy quicksand dream
where you can't move or speak
so your mother scrambles up the steps

on all fours, rushes past you, to the room
where your sister has just now found her voice,
already screaming her story—*it just went off!*
it just went off! —as if a shotgun left to rest

on safety would rise and fire itself.
All this will be hashed and re-hashed around
the supper table, but what stays with you
all these years later, what you cannot forget,

is that moment when your mother
waited at the bottom of the steps
for a word from you—one word—
and all you could offer her was silence.

Response to "Kablooey is the Sound You'll Hear"
from Jacob and Darchel Mohler,
Parents of Brooklynn Mae Mohler and Founders
of the Brooklynn Mae Mohler Foundation

Debra Marquart vividly describes a chilling experience, witnessing the power of a gun—its blast reverberating, the shot forcing its way through matter with no regard for what's in its path, leaving behind the unforgettable scent forever burned into memory. The aftershock brings heavy silence; the mind cannot fathom the unthinkable. The mother desperately waits for some sign, a word. The echo of the blast rings and pulsates in every cell of her body.

Life's normal rhythm of chores and family routine juxtaposes with the gun, casually left out. But now the silence and the thought of her child's death are crushing. This family is able to return to normal life, though changed; they will be haunted forever by *what if.*

The bullet that ripped through our little girl's body at her friend's house extinguished her bright light and drained the life from her. If only the bullet had neglected her body and, instead, destroyed the drywall and paint and spared her life. Our foundation, the Brooklynn Mae Mohler Foundation, works to educate parents on the importance of safe gun storage in the home. We do not want any parent or child living a nightmare they cannot escape.

The Gun Joke

JAMAAL MAY

It's funny, she says, how many people are shocked
by this shooting and the next and next and the next.
She doesn't mean funny as in funny, but funny
as in blood soup tastes funny when you stir in soil.
Stop me if you haven't heard this one:
A young man/old man/teenage boy walks into
an office/theater/daycare/club and empties
a magazine into a crowd of strangers/family/students.

Ever hear the one about the shotgun? What do you call it
when a shotgun tests a liquor store's bulletproof glass?
What's the difference between a teenager
with hands in the air and a paper target charging at a cop?
What do you call it when a man sets his own house on fire,
takes up a sniper position, and waits for firefighters?

Stop me if you haven't heard this one:
The first man to pull a gun on me said it was only a joke,
but never so much as smiled. The second said
this is definitely not a joke, and then his laughter crackled
through me like electrostatic—funny how that works.
When she says it's funny she means funny
as in crazy and crazy as in this shouldn't happen.
This shouldn't happen as in something is off. Funny as in
off—as in, ever since a small caliber bullet chipped his spine,
your small friend walks kinda' funny and his smile is off.

◀ *Response to "The Gun Joke" from* DAN GROSS, *President of the Brady Campaign and Center to Prevent Gun Violence*

I've got another one:

A Republican hunter who loves guns and a Democrat city slicker who doesn't are sitting at the local watering hole somewhere in rural America. The bartender, with a warped sense of humor, brings up "gun control" and sits back to watch the sparks fly—and initially they do. Then, as the two get to talking, they realize they actually agree much more than they disagree, especially about expanding Brady background checks to keep guns out of the hands of people they both agree shouldn't have them, like criminals, domestic abusers, people who are dangerously mentally ill, and terrorists. Then a Congressperson walks into the bar, and the two citizens excitedly share their breakthrough, "Hey, Congressman, guess what! Turns out we've found a solution to gun violence that everyone agrees on and will save lives!" The Congressman responds, "Sorry, guys, doesn't matter. The gun industry is paying my tab."

OK, so this one's not funny either. But you know what would at least be fun? Imagine if we could write a new ending where the Republican and the Democrat get outraged, decide to say #ENOUGH and to hold this Congressman accountable for placing the interests of the gun industry ahead of our safety. Then, in two years, that Congressman is out of a job and needs to buy his own drinks. That's the kind of real change that we all can make through our activism.

Afraid

JILL MCDONOUGH

I'm not afraid of murderers, apparently, or walking alone at
    night,
what I'm supposed to fear. Forty, American, White,

employed: I've already won. But a quick ratty shadow in the
    street,
gunshots breaking air open, doubting what's under my
    feet. . . .

Rachel says *you're afraid of everything* and I flinch because
    she's right.
Heights, rats, gunfire. I'm not afraid of getting shot,

the noise just makes me want to cry. Heights:
not a roof, a bridge, a plane, but ice, ice

skating, ladders, any jolted precarious perch. I remember the
    shim
shaped rock I nicknamed "Lucky" the summer I painted
    houses, gripped

aluminum ladders that telegraphed trembling, ten
bucks an hour. The cheerful song I sang under my breath,

dipping and reaching, keeping everybody safe, ended
he's our Lucky rock his name is Lucky. Then I'd sing it over again.

Response to "Afraid" from KIM PARKER RUSSELL,
Executive Advisor at Women's March, former
Organizing Manager for the Brady Campaign to
Prevent Gun Violence, and Gun Violence Survivor

I sort of remember my life before I became afraid. I was curious, impulsive, and still a little innocent. It's sad for me to realize that time has been gone for almost twenty years now.

Afraid.

That's not hard for me to conjure at all.

I remember my outfit, my hairstyle, my purse, and the springtime air.

I remember the wine I drank and the conversation I had over dinner, much of it about Columbine of all things—it had just happened a few days prior. It was a wonderful evening filled with hope that instantly turned into the worst night of my life.

I remember pleading while running and ducking from flying bullets.

I remember diving under an old truck for cover.

I remember my body feeling like it no longer belonged to me.

I remember trying to play dead while my heart raced fast and hard—it had to be visible, probably gave me away.

I remember feeling a cold, heavy gun pressed onto my head between my eyes.

I remember the shock and confusion when I figured out that I was alive but my friend was not.

Afraid.

I wish I could remember my life before that night with such vivid detail. I miss it. And I miss my friend.

Ballad (American, 21st Century)

WAYNE MILLER

That spring, the shooter was everywhere—
    shot from our minds into the hedgerows,
the pickup beds and second-floor windows,
    the hillocks and tentacled live oaks. And sometimes

he was tracking us with the dilated
    pupil at the tip of his rifle. His bullets spun
into the theater's stop-sign faces, the tessellated
    car lots beyond the exits; they tore holes

in our restaurants and vinyl siding, those fiberglass
    teacups we clamored into at the county fair.
Though you don't remember it, Little Bear,
    a bullet crossed right in front of your car seat—

then window glass covered you like bits
    of clouded ice, and the rain came pouring in
as I raced for shelter at the Wendy's off Exit 10.
    Every night we kept our curtains drawn,

and while your mother slept I sat alone
    in the bathroom dark watching the news surface
into the ice-cut window of my cell phone.
    They said the shooter was in Saint Louis

shooting up a middle school gym, then
    he'd gone to the beach, where he killed a girl
pouring sand from a cup into a sandwich tin.
    (Nevertheless, I pictured his face as a cloud

of insects hovering in the blackest corner
    of the empty lot across the street.) At work
they walked us through scenarios—what to throw
    if he came through my classroom door,

how to arm the students (desks!)
    for counterattack. And when he came—
and when those next four people were erased—
    they trapped him in a high-speed chase

toward the touchless carwash, where the cops
    encircled him and, rather than relent,
he put his rifle barrel to his mouth like the mouth
    of a test tube from some childhood experiment.

◀ *Response to "Ballad (American, 21st Century)" from*
LEE KEYLOCK, *Director of Programs for Narrative 4
and Former Newtown High School Teacher*

"Ballad (American, 21st Century)" terrifies. And it should. Guns kill and they do not discern.

Miller's poem narrows the space between the abstract and the real—removes us from the safety of our La-Z-Boys where we digest the daily news and imagines us into the world of the familiar—"those fiberglass teacups we clamored into at the county fair," perhaps with your grandparents, the "tessellated car lots" where we pre-gamed in our high school jerseys, or outside the "theater's stop-sign faces" where we first learned how to fall in love with girls beyond our reach.

There are no safe havens. The infinite becomes finite. The immaterial becomes material. The intangible tangible. He makes us stare through the "dilated pupil" into our most primal fear: what if it was me?

Four years ago, on 12/14, I sat huddled behind a closed door during lockdown at Newtown High School, in the awful silence, awaiting the terrible texts. The cruel irony of Miller's poem is that there are no "counterattack scenarios" to be "walked through" and not even being safe can save you. Guns kill. No amount of rain pouring through an exploded car window can cleanse this horrifying reality because no cache of bullets has ever stopped to ask how many ways there are to love.

Gun Control: A Triptych

CAROL MUSKE-DUKES

I.

When the older brother, horsing around, opened fire
with the 12 gauge and shot his little brother in the back,
my Aunt Anna pressed her open
hand over the wound, over the blown right lung.
Blood stuttered up
through her fingers. As he began to slide away,
she kept
her hand hard-flat against that death.
At Emergency, they had to pry
it away. He survived that night.
When he takes his shirt off today, at the lake,
you can see the bleach-white stretch where
no hair grows and the skin thins to
her imprint—a hand-span—just under his shoulder
where a wing, if we had wings, might begin to unfurl.

II.

Blood hour. Hour of the startled bird
brought down in a field of first thoughts.
Trigger-quick. You can't know another mind,

but a teacher's job is showing each one how
to remake fate: fluttering up from the nest in
sudden flight. She prints each name in chalk:

each kid waves a wand. Bubbles! Faces
afloat in prisms. Then the one All-Fate, in-
escapable, exploding: camouflage figure, rifle.

Shouting into the room, his shouting mouth.
She has always believed that each soul
confronts the Unknown alone. Now she

sees It loaded, facing her. She calls out their
names, but their cries rise like bird-call, then
descend, one by one. What she's always loved:

their names. And it is almost Story Time, she
dreams, dying. The story today is Blood Hour.

III.
Some say it's High Noon in a big hat, shooting
up the saloon. America? Some say it's your

Second Amendment, those stockpiles of ammo
bought at a chain. Say the next-door kid living in

screen games: exploding heads, walking dead?
Or it's gangs in torched neighborhoods, drugs

running in the brain or a bead drawn on a clinic
doctor, women in line next to a homeless vet,

begging. Some say it's armed revolt, racist cops,
bragging hunters, looter-tools, mass crave/rave

for oblivion: Rapture addicts! Here comes one
more drive-by, school invasion, nightclub terror,

bully/bullied, lynch mob, god cult, toddler-a-cide.
O America, shooting from the hip, from the last of

the trees in a national park, your militia surrounded
by SWAT. Say you're an up-standing patriot in an

invented war—defending unborn lobbyists, a double-
sided coin minted by the National Reprisal Association

of the craven congressionals—saying it to history's
final judge. You, great god Gun, in whom some trust:

in bunker-mind, underground condos. O say it in Homeric
chanted dactyls: I sing of arms & the punk self-pumped-

up lovers of the Silencer. Dickinson wrote it first,
living god of Gun, you are "without the power to die."

Response to "Gun Control: A Triptych" from
Donna Dees-Thomases, *Founder of the*
Million Mom March, Mother's Day 2000—the
Largest Protest Against Gun Violence in US History

I know lots of women just like Aunt Anna.

Some who have saved lives in the literal sense. Like my friend Nancy, a nurse. She went shopping for brussels sprouts at a Tucson Safeway but ended up administering first aid instead. Because of Nancy and the other first responders on the scene, twelve out of the eighteen shot in the attack survived—including Gabby Giffords.

In the metaphorical sense, a sculptor saved the life of Christina-Taylor Green, the youngest to die that January 8, 2011. Christina-Taylor now stands nine feet tall as an angel in a Tucson ball field. A statue with wings and an outstretched hand created from steel salvaged from the wreckage of 9/11 —the day the nine-year-old was born.

I know many metaphorical Aunt Annas, hands-on activists who make indelible imprints on others' lives. Quilters who use fabric from the clothing of slain children. Others who organize sit-ins, lie-ins, lobby days, flash mobs, phone banks, fund raisers, and petition drives. Raise awareness with billboards, boycotts, and gun buybacks. Leading protest marches. Lighting candles. Making ribbons. After each and every shooting. Lifesavers. Every one of them. In their own ways.

In the Dark

JACK MYERS

In memoriam: for my son Jacob Myers, 1985–2009

Anger and sorrow have split off from me
like twin tree trunks. I think I will grow in
opposite directions like this from now on,
watching the fruit of what I can hardly bear open.

When I dared to look at my son's ashes,
I said "focus," but I could not accept that this
was what's left of my boy who, just yesterday,
freshened the world with his jasmine presence.

I would've jumped in front of the bullet, I would've
killed for him, but he was the one who took his life
leaving me swirling in mid-air while the world emptied
itself out and became more meaningless and precious.

I am struck dumb, twisted inward, and folded over
by something so final that I have sworn to stay alive
just to spite death, just so I can stick a thumb in its eye
and then follow through looking for my son in the dark.

Response to "In the Dark" from KHARY PENEBAKER, *2016 Congressional Candidate from Wisconsin and Gun Violence Survivor*

My mom, Joyce, sat in her car, in the dark, alone on the side of the freeway. She put a gun to her head & pulled the trigger. I know her pain, what those dark moments are like. But I also know that my purpose in life is to do everything I possibly can so that no one else has to meet the end of their life at the end of a gun barrel. Call it spite or determination or we can call it inspiration. I have to live the rest of my life without my mom, but there are many ways to prevent others from having to endure that nightmare.

I wish I had the chance to knock on her car window & beg her to put the gun down & struggle & live and hold me rather than that gun. But I can't. What I can do is to help others put theirs down & live & struggle & hold their loved ones & to avoid that empty chair.

I am my mother's voice & I carry a burden that I wouldn't wish on anyone. I carry this burden so fewer people have to.

To Jamyla Bolden of Ferguson, Missouri

NAOMI SHIHAB NYE

Fifty years before you did your homework in Ferguson
we did our homework in Ferguson, thinking life was fair.
If we didn't do our homework we might get a U—
    Unsatisfactory.
Your dad says you didn't even get to see the rest of the world yet.
I've seen too much of the world by now and don't know
how to absorb this—a girl shot through a wall—U! U! U!
I'd give you some of my years if I could—you should not
have died that night—there was absolutely no reason
for you to die. I'd like to be standing in a sprinkler with you,
the way we used to do, kids before air conditioning,
safe with our friends in the drenching of cool,
safe with our shrieks and summer shorts and happy hair,
where can we go without thinking of you now?
Did you know there was a time Ferguson was all a farm?
It fed St. Louis . . . giant meadows of corn, sweet potatoes,
laden blackberry bushes, perfect tomatoes in crates,
and everything was shovels and hoes, and each life,
even the little tendril of a vine, mattered,
and you did your homework and got an S for Satisfactory,
Super, instead of the S of Sorrow now stamped on our hands.

*Response to "To Jamyla Bolden
of Ferguson, Missouri" from*
MISSOURI STATE REPRESENTATIVE
STACEY NEWMAN

I am not a survivor or a victim of gun violence but have a unique responsibility as a public official to prevent others from becoming victims.

It is hard as a mother and grandmother to hear of one more victim somewhere every single day and know that our government has failed to protect other kids like Jamyla. I am often angry and disgusted at the lack of will from my own colleagues in the Missouri state legislature to care enough to put kids first, above the powers of the gun lobby.

My own daughter at age six went on national TV seventeen years ago and talked of her fears of being shot at school. No little kid should even be aware of that danger, but it woke me. Her voice propelled me as an adult to stand on the Missouri House floor and plead for legislators to put kids ahead of firearms, to beg them to care about saving lives. I worry about who will be the next kid shot and killed. I worry about who will be the next Jamyla and know that I must step up my efforts. I must.

Letter Beginning with Two Lines by Czesław Miłosz

MATTHEW OLZMANN

You whom I could not save,
Listen to me.

Can we agree Kevlar
backpacks shouldn't be needed

for children walking to school?
Those same children

also shouldn't require a suit
of armor when standing

on their front lawns, or snipers
to watch their backs

as they eat at McDonalds.
They shouldn't have to stop

to consider the speed
of a bullet or how it might

reshape their bodies. But
one winter, back in Detroit,

I had one student
who opened a door and died.

It was the front
door to his house, but

it could have been any door,
and the bullet could have written

any name. The shooter
was thirteen years old

and was aiming
at someone else. But

a bullet doesn't care
about "aim," it doesn't

distinguish between
the innocent and the innocent,

and how was the bullet
supposed to know this

child would open the door
at the exact wrong moment

because his friend
was outside and screaming

for help. Did I say
I had "one" student who

opened a door and died?
That's wrong.

There were many.
The classroom of grief

had far more seats
than the classroom for math

though every student
in the classroom for math

could count the names
of the dead.

A kid opens a door. The bullet
couldn't possibly know,

nor could the gun, because
"guns don't kill people," they don't

have minds to decide
such things, they don't choose

or have a conscience,
and when a man doesn't

have a conscience, we call him
a psychopath. This is how

we know what type of assault rifle
a man can be,

and how we discover
the hell that thrums inside

each of them. Today,
there's another

shooting with dead
kids everywhere. It was a school,

a movie theater, a parking lot.
The world

is full of doors.
And you, whom I cannot save,

you may open a door
and enter

a meadow or a eulogy.
And if the latter, you will be

mourned, then buried
in rhetoric.

There will be
monuments of legislation,

little flowers made
from red tape.

What should we do? we'll ask
again. The earth will close

like a door above you.
What should we do?

And that click you hear?
That's just our voices,

the deadbolt of discourse
sliding into place.

Response to "Letter Beginning with Two Lines from Czesław Miłosz" from SHANNON WATTS, *Founder of Moms Demand Action for Gun Sense in America*

It took the mass shooting of twenty babies and six educators at an elementary school in Connecticut to wake me up to the reality that gun violence can happen to anyone, anywhere, at any time in America. No one gets out of America unscathed. We all have a story about someone we know who was shot and killed or irreparably injured. And while the details of the victims' stories differ, the outcome is the same: death and destruction.

I didn't choose to get involved in gun violence prevention; I was drafted by a pernicious war that kills more than ninety Americans every day and injures hundreds more. I'm serving as boots on the ground, working side by side with mothers and other women to help stem the tide of lives lost. Babies, toddlers, students, veterans, families—no one is immune to the senseless and sudden toll of a bullet.

And we'll remain on the front lines until, many generations from now, the battle against the insanity of so many guns and so few laws is won by our children and our children's children. But the fight has to start somewhere and, for me, it started in Newtown.

[When a child hears gunshots]

MEGHAN PRIVITELLO

When a child hears gunshots,
she will say *Mom is beating
the pots and pans.* She will say
It sounds like home. Let's keep it
this way; our children
misinterpreting the sound of dying
as a crude percussion.
When they kneel at their beds
and ask God where he was
when their best friend stopped
being alive he will say
*I was at the drive-thru,
I was so hungry I thought the gunshots
were my stomach begging for food.*
He will say *I know nothing
until strangers tell me about it first,
I could have bullet wounds in my hands
and I'd know nothing about what hurts
and doesn't hurt.* What a God; making
the world out of variations of madness,
refusing to hold its face in his hands
and saying *You, you are mine.*
It is not ours: the young blood,
the unfinished drawings,
the last blurry thoughts before a world
goes black. When God is busy wiping grease

from his mouth, we can stand in a line
with the dead in our backpacks,
next to our pencils and our snacks;
he won't notice when
we give the whole damned world back.

◄ *Response to "[When a child hears gunshots]" from* Abbey Clements, *Second-Grade Teacher at Sandy Hook Elementary School on December 14, 2012, and Gun Violence Prevention Activist*

154 shots. They heard them all. I thought they were folding chairs falling. We huddled into the coats and backpacks. Some of them cried. Some of them laughed—how could they know? And if they knew, how could they believe? We shared a water bottle, a blue one, passing it around. Little arms poking out to take it. We waited. We had to believe the police were who they said they were. I opened the door. They scattered. A few in my outstretched arms. We ran. We were lucky. Surviving is a gift and a burden. What do you do with that?

For me, as soon as I could, I started to fight. I fight to keep guns out of the hands of dangerous people. I fight to keep guns locked up and away from curious toddlers and depressed teens. I fight against arming teachers, and I fight to keep guns out of college dorms and classrooms. Lockdowns, active-shooter drills, and backpacks that morph into shields aren't the answer.

Parents shouldn't have to worry about whether or not their kids will make it home from school. A year or two after the tragedy, one mom told me that every day after school she left a gift for her daughter sitting on her bed—a celebration for making it home.

Self-Portrait in Charleston, Orlando

DEAN RADER

The news this morning
said that Ramadi
had fallen to ISIS
and that the president
did not have a plan
to push them back
into the Anbar province
though I have a plan
to walk down to the
beach in silence perhaps
where I will stand
in water the temperature
of most corpses
and look out over
the shapeless ocean—
its waves shifting from
one color to the next,
this moment the shade
of an old bruise—
toward Japan,
which I imagine I see
across the map of
motion, that mystical
country which has

almost completely
rid itself of guns,
like the one the boy
used to shoot nine
people assembled
to worship a man whose
skin history tells us
was the same color
as theirs, that mythical
man who may have walked
the streets of Ramadi in
those missing years
between his youth and
his destiny. And who
knows how many
of the slain
he may have raised
in those streets,
or pulled up out
of night into the
long daylight of the
not-yet-lived,
birthed back into
the skin of suffering,
or how many the man
might have dipped
into those mythical waters
that eventually emptied into
the Gulf of Oman and then
into the Arabian Sea

before their long walk
of waves across
time and history
to South Carolina and
into Charleston
but then retreating to
work their way down
the Eastern coast of
Florida and perhaps
even inland to
Orlando and then
back out again around
every country, every
boat, every body before
arriving on the beaches
of San Francisco on
the far end of the other
side of that mythical
continent, perhaps
even where I am
standing, the water's
color like a bullet, and I
wonder if all life is
somehow loaded into
the chamber of a rifle,
the long tunnel of
darkness before us
our birthright and even
our destiny, all of it
as close to the hammer

as the width of these
lines, themselves an
inheritance of something
I am only now
beginning to understand,
like an insurrection
that no one saw,
not even those
in it, not even the man
with his hand on the trigger
or the people ready to rise.

Response to "Self-Portrait in Charleston, Orlando"
from Joe Quint, *Photographer and Curator of*
It Takes Us *(www.ittakes.us)*

I'll admit that it's easy to get jaded or, more accurately, hardened after working on a project such as mine for a number of years. While all the stories that I've heard from gun violence survivors or the family members of victims are tremendously powerful—each in their own way—they don't affect me in quite the same way as when I began. (If anything, this is a good thing—it allows me to get past my own feelings and hear their stories more clearly.)

The one piece that hasn't changed—and I don't expect that it ever will—is my amazement at the strength and resiliency of these people . . . people who I'm now proud to call friends. For the life of me, I can't understand from where these men and women summon the ability to get out of bed in the morning—and yet they do. I've met people who have become incredible champions for their loved ones and unbelievably effective activists . . . a job they never wanted but wouldn't give up for the world. And I've met people who'll take a total stranger like me to the worst moment in their life for the sake of trying to prevent another family from experiencing their horror.

It's their dedication, inspiration, and sense of purpose that keeps me going. And for that, I am and will always be humbly grateful.

Joe Quint's documentary portrait project, It Takes Us, *takes an honest look at the impact of gun violence on survivors, the family members of victims, and witnesses. View the project and take action at www.ittakes.us.*

Maggot Therapy

ROGER REEVES

Not the debridement of the wound—the wedding
Dress decanted of the bones and snow-blown skin
Of a bride circling through the splinters of winter,
The ash and orchard of a gray heaven surrounding
The tumble of guests leaking out into the night
To wish her sloughing off of dress and wound well—
No, not this debridement, which is greeted with cake
And cymbal and the calling on of a mastering god,
Which is perhaps the dusk erasing itself from day,
The healthy skin of night pulled taut over the bone-
Clots of stars, the chronic fever of noon driven off
Like the fox to the farthest blue hills, the fever kept
There, hidden, hot and vigilant, in the fox's mouth
Which is perhaps the debridement I have been
Looking for—something that will linger inside a suicide
And eat around the bullet still thrumming against
The salt and clatter of the brain which is now below
The bob and tether of an ocean that opens itself
Like a wound, maggot, your mouth, how lightly you travel
Through the ribs of beggars and barns, kings and convents,
How often they've misnamed your benevolence,
Teach me again that I do not own this body
That walks me over this snow and cracked pavement,
The winter light pulling at my bare ankles, teach me
What to do with the dead I carry in my mouth,
Teach me to travel light with their bodies in my belly.

Response to "Maggot Therapy" from
Yvonne Crasso, *Sister of Nina Bradley*
and Gun Violence Prevention Activist

I remember getting a call from my mom. Something had happened with my sister, and my mom had to get home. I hung up with her knowing that my sister was dead. I didn't need to hear it. Yet it all seemed so unreal, so unbelievable. I called my sister's phone until finally the voicemail was full. Such a huge piece of me wanted to believe it wasn't happening. Not to her. Not to us. Then my mom called back. My sister had been shot and she was dead. How could she be dead? She's my sister. She's a mom. She's a daughter.

Through the years my grief has morphed into a new "normal." I've met so many survivors of gun violence along the way. I have learned from them that no one is exempt from gun violence. Not in a school, a theater, or their homes. We all grieve differently, yet we all grieve just the same—we carry our dead with us everywhere we go. With every senseless tragedy, we are reminded of our own and jolted back into the reality of it all.

Years later there are still moments when I am startled by the idea that she is dead. It hits me as if I am just hearing it. The most unreal, inconceivable thing is actually the realest and hardest thing I have ever felt.

The First Child Martyr at Illinois Elementary

LIZ ROSENBERG

Children are so very graceful none
were killed
at Illinois Elementary
when that poor bedeviled woman
emptied her gun on the square-dance floor
—except one boy who stumbled
pushing his friend from the line of fire.
His body should not have been
in that place at that time.
He could not have been more
than eight or nine,
so what did he think about his life to
be so willing to desert it, leaping away
as if to climb ropes in the gym?
He was only a child, falling
like a player on the hardwood floor.
And what on earth did he know

that now we will never know?

That martyred child was where he was supposed to be. He wasn't at the wrong place at the wrong time; the bedeviled woman with the gun was.

Christina-Taylor Green was just nine years old when she was gunned down on a sidewalk in Tucson, the same age as the boy in the poem.

On January 7, about 4:30—a robocall from Gabby Giffords inviting me to her Congress on Your Corner in front of Safeway. On January 8, 10 a.m., Gabby is late; by 10:10 she is nearly dead from gunshots. Two good guys without guns, Roger and Bill, tackle the shooter. I'm flat on the sidewalk against the wall; I can't reach the gun, but I can reach the loaded magazine in his left hand. So I do.

These children are stolen, taken, not lost; we know where the bodies are. When I meet the parents of a murdered child again and again—and the child's age doesn't matter—I don't have any words in my vocabulary to fit the need . . . none.

Some say it's not the gun; it's the shooter. I say it's a very intimate relationship between them. If we had fewer guns in the hands of bedeviled people, we'd have fewer martyrs.

the bullet was a girl

DANEZ SMITH

the bullet is his whole life.
his mother named him & the bullet

was on its way. in another life
the bullet was a girl & his skin

was a boy with a sad laugh.
they say *he asked for it*—

must I define *they*? *they* are not
monsters, or hooded or hands black

with cross smoke.
they teachers, *they* pay tithes

they like rap, *they* police—good folks
gather around a boy's body

to take a picture, share a prayer.
oh da horror, oh what a shame

why'd he do that to himself?
they really should stop
getting themselves killed

Response to "the bullet was a girl" from
THE REVEREND MICHAEL L. PFLEGER,
Pastor of the Faith Community of St. Sabina, Chicago

I have witnessed too many times the other abortion, the one not done in a clinic or a womb but by a society that shapes and molds a person by the denial of basic necessities and opportunities such as a good education, stable housing, food, and a job that allows a person the dignity of taking care of one's self and family.

Yes, too many times I've witnessed the other abortion of poverty, racism, and sexism that has placed a person in the unseen shackles of low self-esteem, and little or no self-love, by a society that has treated you as disposable.

Yes, too many times, I have witnessed the other abortion, where masses of individuals are held hostage in communities that look like third world countries. And the laughter of children has been replaced by the tears of parents. And when a child is asked what they want to be when they grow up, their answer is simply, "Alive." The other abortion that is set up to kill you and then call it suicide.

Yes, the truth is the other abortion is much more prevalent than the one done in a clinic. For many of our children, a bullet has been waiting for them since birth. And while we march against rogue police and self-inflicted genocide that is murdering our children by metal guns, we must also march against, and in fact dismantle, a system that is murdering our children mentally, spiritually, intellectually, and physically every day.

Perhaps the real question is not why are our children getting senselessly killed, but why are we standing by watching?

Undertaker

PATRICIA SMITH

For Floyd Williams

When a bullet enters the brain, the head explodes.
I can think of no softer warning for the mothers
who sit doubled before my desk,
knotting their smooth brown hands,
and begging, *fix my boy, fix my boy*—
here's his high school picture.
And the smirking, mildly mustachioed player
in the crinkled snapshot
looks nothing like the plastic bag of boy
stored and dated in the cold room downstairs.
In the picture, he is cocky and chiseled,
clutching the world by the balls. I know the look.
Now he is flaps of cheek,
slivers of jawbone, a surprised eye,
assorted teeth, bloody tufts of napped hair—
the building blocks of my business.

So I swallow hard, turn the photo face down
and talk numbers instead. The high price
of miracles startles the still-young woman,
but she is prepared. I know that she has sold
everything she owns, that cousins and uncles
have emptied their empty bank accounts,
that she dreams of her baby

in tuxedoed satin, flawless in an open casket,
a cross or blood red rose tacked to his fingers,
his halo set at a cocky angle.
I write a figure on a piece of paper
and push it across to her
while her chest heaves with hoping.
She stares at the number, pulls in
a slow weepy breath. *Jesus.*

But Jesus isn't on this payroll. I work alone
until the dim insistence of morning,
bent over my grisly puzzle pieces, gluing,
sticking, creating a chin with a brushstroke.
I plop glass eyes into rigid sockets,
then carve eyelids from a forearm, an inner thigh.
I plump shattered skulls, and paint the skin
to suggest warmth, an impending breath.
I reach into collapsed cavities to rescue
a tongue, an ear. Lips are never easy to recreate.

And I try not to remember the stories,
the tales of the mothers must bring me
to ease their own hearts. *Oh,* they cry,
my Ronnie, my Willie, my Michael, my Chico.
It was self-defense. He was on his way home,
a dark car slowed down, they must have thought
he was someone else. He stepped between
two warring gang members at a party.
Really, he was trying to get off the streets,
trying to pull away from the crowd.

He was just trying to help a friend.
He was in the wrong place at the wrong time.
Fix my boy—he was a good boy. Make him the way he was.

But I have explored the jagged gaps
in the boy's body, smoothed the angry edges
of bulletholes. I have touched him in places
no mother knows, and I have birthed
his new face. I know he believed himself
invincible, that he most likely hissed
Fuck you, man! before the bullets lifted him
off his feet. I try not to imagine
his swagger, his lizard-lidded gaze,
his young mother screaming into the phone.

She says she will find the money, and I know
this is the truth that fuels her, forces her
to place one foot in front of the other.
Suddenly, I want to take her down
to the chilly room, open the bag
and shake its terrible bounty onto the
gleaming steel table. I want her to see him,
to touch him, to press her lips to the flap of cheek.
The woman needs to wither, finally, and move on.

We both jump as the phone rattles in its hook.
I pray it's my wife, a bill collector, a wrong number.
But the wide, questioning silence on the other end
is too familiar. Another mother needing a miracle.
Another homeboy coming home.

Response to "Undertaker" from
PAMELA BOSLEY, *Mother of Terrell Bosley,*
Cofounder of Purpose Over Pain, Founder
of the Terrell Bosley Anti-Violence Association,
and Violence Prevention Manager at the
Faith Community of St. Sabina in Chicago

My son Terrell Bosley's life was taken at the age of eighteen on the grounds of a church, a place that should have been safe. He was shot once in the shoulder by a .45 caliber, and the bullet traveled internally, destroying his organs. His case remains unsolved like so many other youth in Chicago. Terrell was in his first year of college, working a part-time job, and was very talented. Terrell loved singing and playing the drums and his six-string bass guitar for many great gospel artists. He loved his family and loved being a big brother. Terrell's goal was to graduate from college and to be successful in music. My husband and I did everything to protect Terrell and never would have ever imagined his life being taken. This tragedy really devastated my family. The first year after Terrell's death, I tried to take my life twice and my youngest son at the age of eight prayed that no other person gets shot in his family. My sons, husband, and I cried daily. This is unbearable pain that we will never get over. Our lives will never be the same. No parent should ever have to bury a child.

All the Dead Boys Look Like Me

CHRISTOPHER SOTO

Last time I saw myself die is when police killed Jessie
Hernandez
        A 17–year-old brown queer, who was sleeping
        in their car
Yesterday, I saw myself die again. Fifty times I died in
Orlando. And
        I remember reading, Dr. José Esteban Muñoz
        before he passed
I was studying at NYU, where he was teaching, where he
wrote shit
        That made me feel like a queer brown survival
        was possible. But he didn't
Survive and now, on the dancefloor, in the restroom, on the
news, in my chest
        There are another fifty bodies, that look like
        mine, and are
Dead. And I have been marching for Black Lives and talking
about the police brutality
        Against Native communities too, for years
        now, but this morning
I feel it, I really feel it again. How can we imagine ourselves
// We being black native
        Today, Brown people // How can we imagine
        ourselves
When All the Dead Boys Look Like Us? Once, I asked my
nephew where he wanted

To go to College. What career he would like,
as if

The whole world was his for the choosing. Once, he
answered me without fearing

Tombstones or cages or the hands from a
father. The hands of my lover

Yesterday, praised my whole body. Made the angels from my
lips, Ave Maria

Full of Grace. He propped me up like the roof
of a cathedral, in NYC

Before, we opened the news and read. And read about people
who think two brown queers

Cannot build cathedrals, only cemeteries. And
each time we kiss

A funeral plot opens. In the bedroom, I accept his kiss, and I
lose my reflection.

I am tired of writing this poem, but I want to
say one last word about

Yesterday, my father called. I heard him cry for only the
second time in my life

He sounded like he loved me. It's something I
am rarely able to hear.

And I hope, if anything, his sound is what my body
remembers first.

Response to "All the Dead Boys Look Like Me"
by JOHN GRAUWILER, *Gays Against Guns*
Cofounder and Activist

Christopher Soto's deeply affecting poem is a signpost for understanding the larger LGBTQ/POC experience and its implications; that is, to be queer or a person of color—or both—is to be subject to attack. Soto's poem also explores the effects Orlando has had on our psyches.

My experience with gun violence ranges from personal to witness to affected. I've had a gun pulled on me during a mugging. I've witnessed a person shoot another person, point blank, in the chest. As a teacher, the Sandy Hook massacre shook my faith in humanity. As a person of color, the shooting at the Mother Emmanuel Church in Charleston crushed my soul. As a gay man, Orlando broke my heart.

My rage, coupled with my history of activism, resulted in the forming of Gays Against Guns. After Orlando I found myself with similar-minded LGBTQ people who recognized that complacency was no longer an option. Our community knows opposition intimately. We have run many marathons. Orlando demanded that our community come together and work to fight for a safer America.

Soto's poem reminds us that in spite of the grief we carry from the attacks on our body, a powerful grace exists both in the act of loving and in the act of having love bestowed upon us. Activism is what love looks like in public.

Memory with Handgun and Tetherball

TESS TAYLOR

Portola Middle School they called it.
PMS, we said, feeling so awful often
packed together in our teenage sadness,

finding out the colors of our skins.
In long hallways in classes of 42 students
we learned our codings, locker numbers, gangs.

Mrs Nagsake, Mr Hall, Mrs Theissen, Mrs Mitchell—
the principal with polyester sourbreath:
Our district skidding forward, bankrupt—

our lunches rancid in their plastic
our buses idling in blaring heat.
It seems we still belonged

that year to one another's childhoods
to years we'd shared together and not yet
to wars waged in our names

or to the streets, to guns, or to our futures
to racism poverty or privilege
though they were carving us; we were already carved.

For those months we still circled
the cracked fields, punching our tetherballs.
No textbooks no teachers sometimes no toilet paper:

hull from which some of us headed
nearly immediately to prison
some to private school some to Nation's Burgers—

                    Jabraun, that long lashed boy
who taught me how to use a combination lock
& told me I was pretty for a white girl

shot the next year— now dead two decades.
I can still hear his raspy whisper,
see brown eyes lit like hazel sun.

O all that sweaty suffering:
we danced to Boyz II Men, I sprayed my bangs:
                    I wore my one red guess miniskirt—

        we all fumbled towards one another

            & waited on the bleak tarmac of our lives
            to be let in; to see if we might be let in.
Brash laughter ricochets out to the future.

I lug my dumb survivor's grief.

            O they are tearing down the hull, that school.
            It was always on a landslide zone, a faultline.
            Soon it will be returned to schist hillside.

            Perhaps someone will replant the hillside with
                wildflowers
which the legends say were blooming
when Portola, *conquistador*, came.

Response to "Memory with Handgun and Tetherball" from RENAN SALGADO, *Senior Human Trafficking Specialist at the Worker Justice Center of New York and aka Recording Artist Sai from Demonios Sekt*

Reading Tess Taylor's powerful poem transported me back to that age full of mischief and anxiety known as the Middle School years, a time of transition and uncertainty in terms of your place in the school system (becoming a teenager, but the generic brand not the real one). Growing up in the Brooklyn of the '80s, at the peak of the crack epidemic, these were the years when I first met members of the spectrum of gun violence, from shooters to victims and everything in between. I was twelve when I met the first killer, who was a fifteen-year-old kid from the block who had managed to live by himself thanks to an uncle who signed the lease of his apartment and to the neglect by everyone around. I also saw my first murder victim, eighteen-year-old Willy from my building who lost in a game of handball and didn't want to pay. Today at work, I see through the eyes of twelve-year-old unaccompanied minors who rode on top of commercial trains from Central America, through Mexico, running away from gun violence in their countries, to arrive here, a country also filled with gun violence.

Repeater

ALEXANDRA TEAGUE

Where is the military genius to grasp this terrible engine?
Winchester wrote. This gun that can be loaded
on Sunday and fired all week. This gun that makes a man

*the equal of a company each minute, a regiment in ten,
a full brigade in thirty.* This daylight full of lead—
where is the genius to grasp it? *This terrible engine*

that can sink in a river, fire like it's never been
wet? *A resolute man on horseback* can travel West
for a month of Sundays: this gun makes a man

always ready. So He Cannot Be Captured. No weapon
more effective in the world, its aim more deft.
Where is the military genius to grasp this terrible engine—

to look past its sometimes misfires, its uneven
first trials? To see *like history it repeats itself* (and yes,
sometimes stutters). To fire *the gun* makes a man

almost certain of safety. Against grizzly or Injun,
unequaled. Loaded safe as a church nave. And yet
*where is the military genius to grasp this terrible engine?
Load it on Sunday; fire all week. This gun makes a man.*

Response to "Repeater" from IRAN NAZARIO,
Community Leader and Director of
COMPASS Peacebuilders & Community Relations
at COMPASS Youth Collaborative,
Hartford, Connecticut

I never thought that a gun made a man. I actually had very little experience with guns, and I was never the victim of gun violence as a young man. The most dangerous weapon of all was my education—a series of lessons about the human body and how to make it a weapon. Child abuse, physical abuse, verbal abuse. All ways someone can use their body to impose their will on someone. That was my experience. I grew up believing that hurting people was power and respect. When I immersed myself in the street culture, I learned that street societies live with a different set of rules, and those rules introduced me to the "power" of guns. That line of "education" made power worth more than my own sanity. A gun would lead to my greatest pain. My childhood protector, teenage role model, adult mentor, and eventually my grown-up responsibility—my brother—was murdered. The gun made a man. A sad one, a broken one, a lost one, a forever empty one. That is the man the gun made.

Articulation

NATASHA TRETHEWEY

—after Miguel Cabrera's
portrait of Saint Gertrude, 1763

In the legend, Saint Gertrude is called to write
after seeing, in a vision, the sacred heart of Christ.

Cabrera paints her among the instruments
of her faith: quill, inkwell, an open book,

rings on her fingers like Christ's many wounds—
the heart emblazoned on her chest, the holy

infant nestled there as if sunk deep in a wound.
Against the dark backdrop, her face is a wafer

of light. How not to see, in the saint's image,
my mother's last portrait: the dark backdrop,

her dress black as a habit, the bright edge
of her afro ringing her face with light? And how

not to recall her many wounds: ring finger
shattered, her ex-husband's bullet finding

her temple, lodging where her last thought lodged?
Three weeks gone, my mother came to me

in a dream, her body whole again but for
one perfect wound, the singular articulation

of all of them: a hole, center of her forehead,
the size of a wafer—light pouring from it.

How, then, could I not answer her life
with mine, she who saved me with hers?

And how could I not—bathed in the light
of her wound—find my calling there?

Response to "Articulation"
from EDDIE WEINGART,
Gun Violence Prevention Activist

This poem profoundly resonates with me for a few different reasons, but none more heartbreaking than the familiarity of my mother's then-soon-to-be-ex-husband gunning her down on the evening of February 22, 1981. I was shy of two and a half years old, and her lifeless body fell mere inches away me. As a mother, her instinct was to run to me, to protect me from the man who had abused both of us for over a year and who, in a matter of seconds, would end her life with his 12-gauge shotgun.

I have only three types of memory of my beloved mother: old photographs, the information that family members have taught me about her over the years, and the very graphic flashbacks from that bloody evening—flashbacks that haunt me to this very day. Thirty-six years later I'm still terribly haunted by not knowing the "simple things" about a mother so loving and so willing to risk her life to spare mine. I have absolutely no memory of her voice; I don't know what type of perfume she wore; and though I know in my heart that she told me countless times per day, I have not one memory of hearing my mama tell me that she loves me.

Always & Forever

OCEAN VUONG

Open this when you need me most,
        he said, as he slid the shoe box, wrapped

in duct tape, beneath my head. His thumb,
        still damp from the shudder between mother's

thighs, kept circling the mole above my brow.
        The devil's eye blazed between his teeth

or was he lighting a joint? It doesn't matter. Tonight
        I wake & mistake the bathwater wrung

from mother's hair for his voice. I open
        the shoe box dusted with seven winters

& here, sunk in folds of yellowed news
        -paper, lies the Colt .45 – silent & heavy

as an amputated hand. I hold the gun
        & wonder if an entry wound in the night

would make a hole wide as morning. That if
        I looked through it, I would see the end of this

sentence. Or maybe just a man kneeling
        at the boy's bed, his grey overalls reeking of gasoline

& cigarettes. Maybe the day will close without
          the page turning as he wraps his arms around

the boy's milk-blue shoulders. The boy pretending
          to be asleep as his father's clutch tightens.

The way the barrel, aimed at the sky, must tighten
          around a bullet

to make it speak

I tell you this. There is no language for night bullets. My stepfather shot me with a .306 hunting rifle when I was thirteen years old on the coldest of nights in January in 1970. It cut and sliced its way through my back, leaving shrapnel that still leaves my body. The force ruined a kidney and shocked the nerves in my spine so that I could not walk for months. I resist the language of the "telling" of being shot. Really, this is it. This truth of gun violence in Domestic Violence. First he beat my mother and brother, then, as I became the protector of my family, he took to chasing me along the Connecticut River with his gun and his dog. He leaned in to rape me, and I resisted with fury only available to the knowing of a child. He would take that gun and hang me from a wall night after night. Metal below the chin and pinned. I sit with parents now who have had their child shot. I see the wild-eyed terror of their children the seconds before they were shot. It is terror so visceral that I must tell the truth.

Something It's Taken
Thirty Years to Write

AFAA MICHAEL WEAVER

The door popped open, the bud to yield soft petals
from stems tied to stalks in the dirt, unpainted rails
up under the porch, broken stock of a promise made
before the time to drive over to the 19th Hole
for a drink, the bar where the cowboys break open
swinging doors to sprawl on the street, to settle
card games and jealous blubbering over glasses
of Johnnie Walker Red. Now it is this popping open,

the slack breaking down of two empty pipes where
the shells go like torpedoes, this time the water a kind of air
where children split apart, a sea opened by no kind god
but the angry spit of death determined to kill a day
in spring, to mark it with the pop of shells bursting
in twin tubes of a shotgun here on Milton Avenue,
where there is a church that remembers the tilt
of Easter hats, the Black-is-Proud debate that questioned
the blondness of a thin Jesus too white to love now.

One young black man killing another, an afternoon
when longshoremen changed shifts on Key Highway,
filing across the street by the hundreds with lunches
sliding through their small intestines, or lodged up
somewhere in the colon, the stomach emptying

for what will come at home with a ball game playing,
as if there were no unique day anywhere, except now
in this lifting away. The popping of a shotgun falls
inside the whistle of cargo trains heading west
under shrill wishes of seagulls with invisible feathers.

◀ *Response to "Something It's Taken Thirty Years to Write" from* LEANA S. WEN, MD, MSC, *Commissioner of Health for the City of Baltimore*

There are those who question that violence is a public health issue. I wonder if they have seen the impact of violence on individuals, families, and their communities. As an emergency physician, I have resuscitated young men dying of gunshot injuries, children caught in the crossfire, and babies and vulnerable older adults who suffer from abuse and neglect. I have seen how violence maims and kills and forever impacts a person's health and well-being.

Scientific studies show that violence spreads from person to person, just like other communicable diseases. Just like other diseases, violence has a treatment and a cure. And it can be prevented, using the same public health approaches we take to other diseases.

First, we must stop violence where it occurs. In Baltimore, our Safe Streets program employs individuals—many of whom are returning citizens—to walk the streets and mediate conflicts. In one year, our outreach workers stopped over seven hundred conflicts. Second, we must recognize the link between violence and trauma. It is hurt people who hurt people. Every interaction is a point of intervention, and we must improve mental health and substance addiction treatment and address systemic trauma. Third, we must invest in our young people. In Baltimore, we see lead poisoning prevention and getting glasses to children as violence prevention strategies. Taking a public health approach to violence is how we can ensure that where our children live no longer determines whether they live.

Kalashnikov Candelabrum

ROBERT WRIGLEY

*for Mark Solomon & the Peace Art Project,
Cambodia, 2004*

There being no art supplies in the nation,
the government of Cambodia donated
thousands of decommissioned Kalashnikovs
to the visiting artists, and it was with those
death machines—disassembled, bent, reshaped
from what they were into what they were not—
that they taught the children to make flowers,
chairs, and tables; elephants, miraculous fish
and other mythical beasts. As well as this elegant
black steel candelabrum, brought all the way
from Cambodia to a mountaintop in Idaho,
from its relentless fire to these five mild candles,
burning again and again and again and again,
and yet again, for our lost American lives.

Response to "Kalashnikov Candelabrum"
from JESSICA POLLACK MINDICH,
Founder of the Caliber Collection and
President of the Caliber Foundation

Art creates change. It has the power to heal, inspire, teach, and unite. In my work, art provides me with a platform to bring awareness to the disparity of impact among populations in America—the reality that African Americans make up only 12 percent of the US population but they account for 50 percent of all homicide victims. I am a jewelry designer determined to make an impact on gun violence in America.

I created a series of cuffs, bracelets, and cufflinks engraved with the serial numbers from illegal guns and created with the metal from shell casings that have been swept from crime scenes or turned over through gun buyback and amnesty programs. By transforming these instruments of destruction into jewelry and donating a portion of the sales proceeds to fund gun buyback and amnesty programs, the Caliber Collection creates a virtuous cycle of hope. The power of guns has always been associated with the hand of a shooter. Now people can use guns to make peace.

My work is completely apolitical. With jewelry, we have been able to neutralize the emotions that rage over the word "guns" and engage citizens from all over the world in the process of peace. Supporters from more than eighty-seven countries have contributed to our efforts to make our streets and homes safer.

The editors would like to express our deepest gratitude to the following people for their contributions to this project. Without you, this project would not have reached this point:

Colum McCann and Lisa Consiglio of Narrative 4; Helene Atwan and all the staff of Beacon Press; Sarah Clements; Abbey Clements; Laura Maloney and Misha Lehrer of Senator Murphy's office; Rob Spillman; Richard Nash; Shannon Watts; Lucy McBath; Rob Casper; Carolyn Baccaro; Billy Joe Mills; Georgette Brown at the Brady Campaign and Center; and all the poets and respondents in this book.

We also wish to express our ongoing commitment to honor the millions of victims and survivors of American gun violence and their families in the fight to eradicate gun violence in this country. Follow additional content, information, and interviews at www.beacon.org/bulletsintobells and in the many events to come around the country in the months following publication of this anthology.

CREDITS

Nick Arnold, "Jordan." Copyright © 2017 by Nick Arnold.

Jimmy Santiago Baca, "Morning Shooting." Copyright © 2017 by Jimmy Santiago Baca.

Aziza Barnes, "I Could Ask, But I Think They Use Tweezers." Copyright © 2017 by Aziza Barnes.

Reginald Dwayne Betts, "When I Think of Tamir Rice While Driving." Copyright © 2017 by Reginald Dwayne Betts.

Richard Blanco, "One Pulse—One Poem." Copyright © 2017 by Richard Blanco.

Tara Bray, "How My Mother Died," from *Mistaken for Song*. Copyright © 2009 by Tara Bray. Reprinted with the permission of the publishers, Persea Books, Inc. (New York), www.perseabooks.com. All rights reserved.

Jericho Brown, "Bullet Points." Copyright © 2017 by Jericho Brown.

Brian Clements, "22." Copyright © 2017 by Brian Clements.

"Boy Shooting at a Statue" from *The Trouble with Poetry: And Other Poems* by Billy Collins, copyright © 2005 by Billy Collins. Used by permission of Random House, an imprint and division of Penguin Random House LLC. All rights reserved.

Kyle Dargan, "Natural Causes." Copyright © 2017 by Kyle Dargan.

Joel Dias-Porter, "Wednesday Poem." Copyright © 2017 by Joel Dias-Porter.

Natalie Diaz, "Catching Copper." Copyright © 2017 by Natalie Diaz.

Mark Doty, "In Two Seconds." Copyright © 2017 by Mark Doty.

"Meditation at Fifty Yards, Moving Target" from *American Smooth*, W.W. Norton & Company, New York, NY. © 2004 by Rita Dove. Reprinted by permission of the author.

Cornelius Eady, "Gun Poem." Copyright © 2017 by Cornelius Eady.

"Heal the Cracks in the Bell of the World" from *Vivas to Those Who Have Failed: Poems* by Martín Espada. Copyright © 2015 by Martín Espada. Used by permission of W.W. Norton & Company, Inc.

Tarfia Faizullah, "Aubade with Lemon and Sage." Copyright © 2017 by Tarfia Faizullah.

Jameson Fitzpatrick, "A Poem for Pulse." Copyright © 2017 by Jameson Fitzpatrick.

Nick Flynn, "My Mother Contemplating Her Gun," from *Some Ether*. Copyright © 2000 by Nick Flynn. Reprinted with the permission of the Permissions Company, Inc., on behalf of Graywolf Press, Minneapolis, Minnesota, www.graywolfpress.org.

Rebecca Morgan Frank, "Gunning for It," from *Sometimes We're All Living in a Foreign Country*. Copyright © 2017 by Rebecca Morgan Frank. Reprinted with the permission of the Permissions Company, Inc., on behalf of Carnegie Mellon University Press, www.cmu.edu/universitypress.

Ross Gay, "The Bullet, in Its Hunger," from *Against Which*. Copyright © 2006 by Ross Gay. Reprinted with the permission of the Permissions Company, Inc., on behalf of CavanKerry Press, Ltd., www.cavankerry.org. All rights reserved.

Vanessa German, "[11 Gunshots]." Copyright © 2017 by Vanessa German.

Robert Hass, "Dancing." Copyright © 2017 by Robert Hass.

Juan Felipe Herrera, "Poem by Poem," from *Notes on the Assemblage*. Copyright © 2015 by Juan Felipe Herrera. Reprinted with the permission of the Permissions Company, Inc., on behalf of City Lights, www.citylights.com.

Bob Hicok, "Throwing a Life Line." Copyright © 2017 by Bob Hicok.

Brenda Hillman, "The Family Sells the Family Gun." Copyright © 2017 by Brenda Hillman.

"Those Who Cannot Act" from *After: Poems* by Jane Hirshfield. Copyright © 2006 by Jane Hirshfield. Courtesy of HarperCollins Publishers.

LeAnne Howe, "Gatorland." Copyright © 2017 by LeAnne Howe.

Major Jackson, "Ferguson." Copyright © 2017 by Major Jackson.

Michael Klein, "The Talking Day." Copyright © 2017 by Michael Klein.

Yusef Komunyakaa, "Shotguns." Copyright © 2017 by Yusef Komunyakaa.

Dana Levin, "Instructions for Stopping." Copyright © 2017 by Dana Levin.

Ada Limón, "The Leash." Copyright © 2017 by Ada Limón.

Deborah Marquart, "Kablooey is the Sound You'll Hear," from *Small Buried Things*. Copyright © 2015 by Deborah Marquart. Reprinted with the permission of the Permissions Company, Inc., on behalf of New Rivers Press, www.newriverspress.com.

Jamaal May, "The Gun Joke." Copyright © 2017 by Jamaal May.

Jill McDonough, "Afraid," from *Reaper*. Copyright © 2017 by Jill McDonough. Reprinted with the permission of the Permissions Company, Inc., on behalf of Alice James Books, www.alicejamesbooks.org.

"Ballad (American, 21st Century)" from *Post: Poems* by Wayne Miller (Minneapolis: Milkweed Editions, 2016). Copyright © 2016 by Wayne Miller. Reprinted with permission from Milkweed Editions. www.milkweed.org.

Carol Muske-Dukes, "Gun Control: A Triptych." Copyright © 2017 by Carol Muske-Dukes.

Jack Myers, "In the Dark," from *The Memory of Water*. Copyright © 2011. Reprinted with the permission of New Issues Press.

Naomi Shihab Nye, "To Jamyla Bolden of Ferguson, Missouri." Copyright © 2017 by Naomi Shihab Nye.

Matthew Olzmann, "Letter Beginning with Two Lines by Czesław Miłosz." Copyright © 2017 by Matthew Olzmann.

Meghan Privitello, "[When a child hears gunshots]." Copyright © 2017 by Meghan Privitello.

Dean Rader, "Self Portrait in Charleston, Orlando," from *Self-Portrait as Wikipedia Entry*. Copyright © 2017 by Dean Rader. Reprinted with the permission of the Permissions Company, Inc., on behalf of Copper Canyon Press, www.coppercanyonpress.org.

Roger Reeves, "Maggot Therapy," from *King Me*. Copyright © 2013 by Roger Reeves. Reprinted with the permission of the Permissions Company, Inc., on behalf of Copper Canyon Press, www.coppercanyonpress.org.

"The First Child Martyr at Illinois Elementary" from *Children of Paradise*, by Liz Rosenberg, © 1994. Reprinted by permission of the University of Pittsburgh Press.

Danez Smith, "the bullet was a girl." Copyright © 2017 by Danez Smith.

Patricia Smith, "Undertaker," from *Close to Death*. Copyright © 1998. Reprinted with the permission of Zoland Books, an imprint of Steerforth Press.

Christopher Soto, "All the Dead Boys Look Like Me." Copyright © 2017 by Christopher Soto.

Tess Taylor, "Memory with Handgun and Tetherball." Copyright © 2017 by Tess Taylor.

Alexandra Teague, "Repeater," from *The Wise and Foolish Builders* (Persea). Copyright © 2017 by Alexandra Teague.

Natasha Trethewey, "Articulation." Copyright © 2017 by Natasha Trethewey.

Ocean Vuong, "Always & Forever," from *Night Sky with Exit Wounds*. Copyright © 2016 by Ocean Vuong. Used with the permission of the Permissions Company, Inc., on behalf of Copper Canyon Press, www.coppercanyonpress.org.

Afaa Michael Weaver, "Something It's Taken Thirty Years to Write." Copyright © 2017 by Afaa Michael Weaver.

Robert Wrigley, "Kalashnikov Candelabrum." Copyright © 2017 by Robert Wrigley.

GABRIELLE GIFFORDS and MARK KELLY: Following the tragedy at Sandy Hook Elementary School, former congresswoman Gabrielle Giffords and her husband, Navy combat veteran and NASA astronaut Captain Mark Kelly, founded Americans for Responsible Solutions to encourage elected officials to stand up for solutions to prevent gun violence, protect responsible gun ownership, and make communities safer. Congresswoman Giffords was shot in 2011 during a "Congress on Your Corner" event while representing Arizona's Eighth Congressional District.

COLUM MCCANN is the author of *TransAtlantic, Let the Great World Spin*, and *Thirteen Ways of Looking*.

BRIAN CLEMENTS is the author of multiple books, most recently *A Book of Common Rituals*, and editor of *An Introduction to the Prose Poem*. He lives in Newtown, Connecticut, where his wife, a teacher, survived the Sandy Hook Elementary School shooting.

ALEXANDRA TEAGUE is the author of *Mortal Geography*, winner of the California Book Award for Poetry, and *The Wise and Foolish Builders*. Alexandra is an associate professor of poetry at the University of Idaho.

DEAN RADER is the author of *Self-Portrait as Wikipedia Entry* and editor of *99 Poems for the 99 Percent: An Anthology of Poetry*. He lives in San Francisco.

▶ Please visit www.beacon.org/bulletsintobells
for poet biographies.